THE REAL PEOPLE OF WIND AND RAIN

OTHER WORKS BY ANDREW SCHELLING

Claw Moraine (1987)

Ktaadn's Lamp (1991)

Dropping the Bow: Poems from Ancient India (1991, revised 2008)

Moon Is A Piece Of Tea (1993)

For Love of the Dark One: Songs of Mirabai (1993, revised 1998)

The India Book (1993)

Old Growth: Selected Poems & Notebooks 1986-1994 (1995)

Songs of the Sons & Daughters of Buddha (with Anne Waldman, 1996)

The Cane Groves of Narmada River (1998)

The Road to Ocosingo (1998)

Tea Shack Interior: New & Selected Poetry (2001)

Wild Form, Savage Grammar (2003)

Erotic Love Poems from India: A Translation of the Sanskrit Amaruśataka (2004)

Two Elk: A High Country Notebook (2005)

Kamini (2007)

Old Tale Road (2008)

From the Arapaho Songbook (2011)

A Possible Bag (2013)

EDITING

Jimmy & Lucy's House of "K" #1-9 (with Benjamin Friedlander)

Dark Ages Clasp the Daisy Root #1-9 (with Benjamin Friedlander)

Disembodied Poetics: Annals of the Jack Kerouac School (with Anne Waldman, 1996)

The Wisdom Anthology of North American Buddhist Poetry (2005)

The Oxford Anthology of Bhakti Literature (2011)

Love & the Turning Seasons: India's Poetry of Spiritual & Erotic Longing (2014)

THE
REAL PEOPLE
OF WIND
AND RAIN

Andrew Schelling

Talks, Essays, & an Interview

Singing Horse Press

2014

Singing Horse Press
5251 Quaker Hill Lane
San Diego, CA 92130

ACKNOWLEDGMENTS

Thanks to the editors & readers of the print journals, on-line sites, and books, where these writings appeared. Thanks also to the poets of Orono, Maine, and the scholars and artists in Delhi, who invited me to their conferences. "Post Coyote at Orono" was a talk at the University of Maine, Orono, in 2008 for the National Poetry Foundation's "American Poetry in the 1970s." It appeared in *Jacket #36* and on the website of Bob & Susan Arnold's Longhouse, 2008. § "Over the River Again": *Pacific Rim Review of Books #2*. Reprinted in *con / crescent I: a biannual journal of the arts*, Fall 2009. § "Buddhism & the Precepts of Baseball": *Shambhala Sun*, December 2003. § "The Real People of Wind & Rain": introduction to Joanne Kyger, *Lo & Behold: Household & Threshold on California's North Coast*. Voices from the American Land, Winter 2009. § "Salvage Ethnopoetics & the Songs of the Gāhā-Kosa": *Mandorla #13*, 2010. § "Oil & Wolves": symposium guest edited by Jonathan Skinner for *Interim*. Issue 29: Ecopoetics, 2011. § "A View from North America: Mirabai" was presented at Delhi University for a panel organized by Ms. Ira Raja in 2007. "Lal Ded": fold-out chapbook from Longhouse, 2008; posted on Jerome Rothenberg's Poems & Poetics blogsite, August 3, 2009. "Jayadeva": limited edition artist's book, *Kamini: Poems from Jayadeva's Gīta-govinda*. Emdash Editions, 2007. All three selections in Mānoa 22:2, Wild Hearts: Literature, Ecology, and Inclusion. § "The Beat Scene Interview with Trevor Carolan": *Beat Scene #44*, 2003. § "The Songs of Jaime de Angulo": *Home Among the Swinging Stars: Collected Poems of Jaime de Angulo*, La Alameda Press, 2006. § "Towards Arcturus": privately printed at La Alameda Press, 2007.

I also want to thank the following individuals. JB Bryan for early post-coyote thoughts in *Gourd 2*, focused conversations, and an exemplary eye to book design. Tim Hogan, ecology insight, & companionship in the search for Indian Peaks game drive walls. Keith Abbott for his baseball sumi-e. Smt. Vidya Rao for a singer's insight into bhajan and thumri song styles. Kika Silva for her translations. Paul Naylor, friend and publisher, for sharp suggestions that made the book better. And Rebecca Eland, for support and careful comments throughout.

CONTENTS

For Thomas & Alice (Alinka) Schelling
first the land, then books—

The whole drama of Karok life takes place in a world
of rivers and ridges. They move in terms of "up-ridge"
and "down-ridge", "up-stream" and "down-stream", and
have no concern with "north" "south" "east" and "west".
Even their linguistic concepts seem to reflect
the nature of the land they live in.

JAIME DE ANGULO

Might take bird books on trip.

LORINE NIEDECKER

COYOTE'S JOURNAL

Cover, Coyote's Journal 5/6 (1966)

POST COYOTE AT ORONO

FOR AT LEAST FIFTY YEARS AN UNNAMED SCHOOL has persisted in North American poetry—a school that is not a school, its members largely disinterested in membership in any academy. This loose gathering of poets does not much factor in popular or scholarly discussions of the current "post-avant" poetry scene, which I consider a loss because it shares recognizable roots with the experimentalists in what I regard as the great consolidations of the 1970s. I'd like to give some definition to these shadowy, across-the-border poets by detailing a few of their salient characteristics.

Tongue partly in cheek—and because these days nearly everything gets labeled "post"—I will call these writers Post Coyote. This is first in reference to a fine enterprise, *Coyote's Journal*, which began publication in 1964 and which has reemerged in one form or another up to the present. Behind the original journal's pages steps the fugitive figure of coyote, a North American culture hero, and his surprisingly resilient progeny. Nobody should ignore this creature's success as a scavenger from the West Coast manzanita scrub, through the continent's high-plains heartland, to the sugarbush of Vermont[1].

For those who live in non-urban American settings, the coyote's ululation has long been a cultural and emotional equivalent to the Japanese cherry tree, able to elicit complicated emotions and a bank of half-spoken images. Didn't Philip Whalen once write from Kyoto, "an entire civilization built on an inarticulate response to cherry blossoms"?

Well, *Coyote's Journal* did little publishing in the 1970s. Its main impact occurred in the mid to late sixties, but the poetics it stood for came into sharpest focus through the seventies. Post Coyote poets, bringing the discoveries and recoveries of the 1970s forward into the twenty-first century, share with each other a number of touchstone interests and social or spiritual reference points. Most visibly, these poets lean towards a carefully thought out land ethic (Aldo Leopold's term) & a decentralized approach to community or government. Their general identification with bioregion, rather than nation-state or *Internationale*, as well as their general avoidance of academic life, may account for the group's invisibility; or when noticed, the supposition that they operate as mavericks, loners, or eccentrics. I'm going to speak to a few Post Coyote qualities or streams of influence, by tracking the writings into some important publications. Let me begin with a bit of personal history since I don't think this incidental.

The first and only time I signed up for a poetry course in college was spring semester, 1974. I'd arrived at U.C. Santa Cruz in January, the day after an uncharacteristic snowfall shut down the Coast Range mountains, and I enrolled in Norman O. Brown's class called simply "Introduction to Poetry." Brown at the outset of his career had been a left-leaning Classics professor. He published a forward-looking Marxist analysis of Greek mythology in 1947, *Hermes the Thief*, then a book that set Freud the task of filling in a truckload of things Marx had missed, *Life Against Death*. Most specifically, through Freud Nobby (N.O.B.) found a clue to how people, mental states, and historical periods return again and again—maybe a return of the repressed, but equally a principle of metaphor, or metamorphosis.

At the end of *Life Against Death*, having come to a realization that poetry was the singular way forward, both politically and spiritually, Brown turned during the sixties to an aphoristic form of writing—a form "... so perishable that it cannot be hoarded by any elite or stored in any institution." Much of his writing he collaged from Freud, Blake, the Western Gnostic traditions, H.D., Ezra Pound, Vedanta texts, & Taoism. With these he produced his defining book, 1966's *Love's Body*. His literary influences seemed to be Ezra Pound, possibly the Pre-Socratics, and more ambiguously Robert Duncan, who evidently baffled him. Brown was a contributor to Clayton Eshleman's journal *Caterpillar*, was a close friend & thorny critic of John Cage, a correspondent and briefly the lover of M.C. Richards, and knew Duncan personally and his writings well.[2]

14

Brown's course: Ten of us met once a week, three hours, in a small meadow
fringed by redwoods, near historic nineteenth century lime kilns on the Santa Cruz
campus. Brown assigned two books—Jerome Rothenberg's grand postmodern-
primitive assemblage, *Technicians of the Sacred*, and the North American anthology
Rothenberg had co-edited with George Quasha, *American A Prophecy*, published the
year before and just out in paperback.

Brown was a bit of a coyote himself, an armature of contradictory impulses—
warmhearted, then coldly aloof; deadly literalist and more deadly with puns; pas-
sionately engaged, then prophetically far off; gently considerate with undergraduates,
impatient and at times hostile towards graduate students; a book-obsessed scholar,
a man who loathed bookishness. We mostly read poetry aloud, concentrating on the
physical qualities of phonemes, syllables, words, lines. He encouraged us to recite
orally, letting our bodies set the rhythm, and to shy from explanation or paraphrase.
We memorized poems—versions from the Gabon Pygmy, Tamil, Hopi, or Chippewa, as
well as poems by North American contemporaries. Mostly we lingered over poems that
revealed "the law of metamorphosis." Brown held this to be the root of poetry.

> The fish does ... HIP
> The bird does ... VISS
> The marmot does ... GNAN
>
> I throw myself to the left,
> I throw myself to the right,
> I act the fish ...

Among the poems that have stayed with me thirty years, and become part of my toolkit, is this song by the Ojibwa singer Mary English, collected & translated by
Frances Densmore—

a loon
I thought it was
but it was
my love's
splashing oar

Another from Densmore's Ojibwa (Chippewa), a dream song by Ajidegijig, has the flavor of Japanese haiku, yet is located in a Plains culture that knew nothing of Bashō or Buson.

as my eyes
search
the prairie
I feel the summer in the spring

What I want to emphasize is that an entry to poetry through Rothenberg's and Quasha's anthologies—the only formal training I received in college—from a scholar-poet whose work was appearing in the far-reaching journal *Caterpillar*—was one where Frances Densmore's versions of Teton Sioux songs (a single word of Sioux entered as a sharply pronounced line in English) got placed alongside the abrupt stops & starts of Robert Creeley. Ishmael Reed appeared against an Aztec codex; Gertrude Stein abutted a Papago Indian naming ceremony. My first Denise Levertov poem, never forgotten, was a translation from Aztec by way of Spanish.

The artist: disciple, abundant, multiple, restless.
The true artist: capable, practicing, skillful;
maintains dialogue with his heart, meets things with his mind.

The epigram that held everything in place came as a bolt from someplace I knew must exist but had never seen. Ezra Pound—

It is dawn at Jerusalem while midnight hovers above the Pillars of Hercules. All ages are contemporaneous in the mind.

These were signature moments, opening a poetry neither nationalist in outlook, restricted to a single language, nor up-to-date. It was raw, physical, cross-cultural, multilingual. By the time I found Donald Allen's *The New American Poetry* some years later—a justly praised book I knew had formed the brave world I was entering—it seemed quite square, limited in scope, restricted in geography, ethnicity, culture, and language. That book full as it was of heroes could never raise the excitement of Rothenberg's project—spurred by translation, ethnographic fieldwork, a sense of the world's watersheds, linguistics, and a far-flung geographic imagination. "The power of a live tradition to 'make new' whatever in the past can grow in the present," is how Rothenberg put it: and the poet's task to document "lines of recovery & discovery."

These lines of recovery and discovery did not just mean poetry either. Rothenberg sets out the work of archaeologists, linguists, healers, anthropologists, historians, vision seekers, translators, as part of the project. I would add geographers, botanists, and ecologists, people who form a subtle skin underneath the work of those others. The move towards bioregionalism, a key stance of Post Coyote-ism, was already in motion, though not yet named. Dale Pendell, a good poet, a heroic ethnobotanist, & a trickster historian, took his less known but profoundly instructive journal *Kyoi* in 1974 and renamed it *Kuksu*. 1978's issue #4 opens with an editor's note—

Kuksu (formerly *Kyoi*) works with regional emphases. While we concentrate on rural Northern California, we try to include representatives of associated areas across the continent and around the world. Glancing back over past issues, perhaps what we mean by "representatives of associated areas" are individuals who by evidence of their writing would feel themselves to be, if not at home, at least comfortable guests in the Northern California backcountry. We feel that the geographical space delineated by the occurrence of "Kuksu cults" in the early twentieth century and before, forms, still, a resonant cultural aggregate sharing rivers, climate, flora and fauna, patterns-of-speech, pioneering history, ecological problems, contemporary social and political "initiations," and aboriginal mythology. It is from the latter category that comes the unifying culture-bearer 'Kuksu,' our namesake.[3]

Change a few words and you could apply Pendell's editorial stance to classical Tamil poetry anthologies, the Chinese *Shih Ching*, Hopi oral narrative, or Haida myth-telling. Northern California's (*Kuksu's*) huge diversity of native languages plus its position on the Pacific Rim—which meant large numbers of Spanish, Chinese and Japanese immigrants who'd been there longer than most of the Euro-Americans, and eventually Hmong, Vietnamese, and Cambodian refugees—make the coast a necessary site for translation. It is geographically and imaginatively proximate to Asia. Salmon in the creeks, bear in the mountains, ten thousand years of shared technology and oral poetry winding up from San Diego to Haida Gwai, across the Bering Strait, down to Sakhalin Island, Hokkaido, and Okinawa.

From a literary point of view it was in the wake of Pound, Witter Bynner, Kenneth Rexroth, and post-War II poets Cid Corman and Gary Snyder, that dozens of American poets settled in to learn an Asian language, or relocated to Taipei or Beijing to study the Classics.[4] From a geographic and pragmatic point of view this turn towards Asian language study would have become necessary anyhow, and much was spurred by the Indochina War. Many poets with East Asian experience as journalists, teachers, monks, scholars, or travelers, later settled on the West Coast of America. The Olympic Peninsula is just one notable enclave.[5]

A few years ago I wrote a sentence I still stand by: "If I open a magazine of contemporary poetry I rarely hear John Dryden, but almost always Li Bo."

California was not the only place a backcountry stance took hold during the seventies. I want to mention Bob & Susan Arnold's Longhouse, a publishing venture that has produced hundreds of books, cards, and journals issuing from backwoods Vermont over the last four decades. In an early editor's note Arnold says, "Longhouse has published poetry from the Green River since 1973—we are also interested in publishing travel journals and prose concentrating on back country life and attitude." Longhouse every year brings into print a huge range of writers, but Bob and Susan test the legitimacy of poems against their physical chores in the back woods, while the numerous translations of East Asian and South Asian poetry they've issued cannot be ignored.

I'm going to step outside poetry for a moment, & make a historical observation about what set up some of the "lines of discovery" that appear in Rothenberg's anthologies, *Coyote's Journal*, and so forth. Some of them feed directly into "back country life & attitude," others are so much part of North American history they sometimes seem invisible: modern game management techniques; the Boasian project of language and culture salvage; scientific forestry; the emergent field of ecology; the electric guitar (earliest documented use, 1932, Wichita, Kansas); Carbon 14 dating techniques (1949); the typewriter with QWERTY keyboard; paperback books as affordable items. These are all Modernist gestures that emerge along the same timeline as poetry. All congeal around poetry in the 1970s. They reaffirm on new foundations the old beliefs in animal magic, plant lore, erotic love as a gateway to knowledge, and the power of both human & animal voices and bodies.

The single magazine that to my thinking could capture the Seventies bioregional ethos would be *Coyote's Journal*. Edward van Aelstyn, William Wroth, and James Koller founded it in 1964, from the ashes of a suppressed issue of the *Northwest Journal*. The *Northwest* had been published under the aegis of the University of Oregon, but administrators killed it after citizens expressed outrage over an interview with Fidel Castro, and Antonin Artaud's ferocious poem "To Have Done With the Judgment of God."

The Modernist discoveries I listed a moment ago give scope to *Coyote's Journal* from its beginnings, and you can see them without even breaking the covers open.

Travel light

Pleasing smell of
sea urchins and sweet potatoes
Around the burning driftwoods.

In East china sea.
On the beach of a tiny island
I find myself
sitting in a cave.
With a hundred human skulls
who died by the small pox
Three hundred years ago.

One by one
I listen to their stories
All night long.

As the rosy dawn streaks
One of them mumbles

"To travel light
why don't you leave your skull here?"

Nanao

Poem by Nanao Sakaki, rear cover Coyote's Journal 11 (1987)

The earliest issue I own is 1966's #5-6. Its front cover reproduces a 1905 photograph
(black & white) by naturalist Herman T. Bohlman: a coyote (*Canis latrans*) in close-up,
peering through high stem prairie grasses in Oregon. The extraordinary cool intelligence in the coyote's face is what makes the photo irresistible. The issue itself includes
Projectivist poems by Snyder, Whalen, Kyger, some early Clark Coolidge, and a chapter
of Robert Duncan's *H.D. Book*.

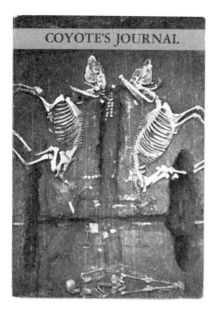

From its first issue, *Coyote's Journal* always placed a handwritten facsimile or block print poem on its rear cover. The effect of this was to emphasize the period's belief in poetry as a physical act and the poem itself as an object, a thing made, not just an idea or a voice, but a piece of craft, no less solid than a burr-wood table. Similarly the journal's interest in concrete poetry, as well as "sound poetry" or verse built on non-lexical (nonsense) voicing, gave added emphasis to eye, ear, hand, throat, heart.

Let me mention another cover photo. *Coyote's Journal* issue #8 (1967): "Chariot Burial, Anyang, Hunan Province." The black & white image is credited to the Chinese People's Association for Cultural Relations with Foreign Countries. It documents an excavated burial, two horse skeletons lying back to back in a square pit, a human skeleton laid crosswise about a horse's length behind. The human's breastbone is nestled into the sod, skull turned restully over its left shoulder. Coins, harnesses, yokes, weapons, and other necessary items for the ride to the next world lie among the skeletal remains. The human is what remains of a once-proud warlord. In a clear rhyme with the cover, a Charles Olson poem opens the issue with five sharp breaths, each built on phonetics of the previous line—

rages

strain

Dogs of Tartarus

Guards of Tartarus

Finks of the Bosses, War Makers[6]

Coyote's

Journal

Twenty years later, three issues farther on, *Coyote's Journal* #11 (1987)—(we've leapfrogged the nineteen-seventies)—held on its cover another black & white photograph, taken by Owen Lattimore in Chinese Mongolia, 1935: "The 'coffin' of Chinghis Khan being loaded on a ceremonial cart." This issue opens with forty pages of Chinese and Mongolian poems in translation by Gary Snyder, Burton Watson, Sam Hamill, and German *compadre* Stefan Hyner, then poems by Japanese World War II veteran & counterculture icon Nanao Sakaki. Eighty pages later the same issue closes with 35 pages of "New Works from Europe" (concrete poems, collages, edgy snapshots, holograph scores, incantations) edited by Swiss poet Franco Beltrametti, a close friend of many postmodern primitive, back country, anarchist, communalist North American poets. These two sections of the journal bookend us, the North Americans: *We are the West*. Asia and Europe cradle us.

A large number of contemporary Native American poets show up in *Coyote's Journal*: Wendy Rose, Simon Ortiz, Peter Blue Cloud, Harold Littlebird, Joy Harjo, Nettie Reuben, and others. The ancestral regard the editors show Asia and Europe is balanced with a personal regard shown indigenous America. An important shift occurred on *CJ's* cover from 1967 to 1987—from Imperial China to "Chinese Mongolia." (Inner Mongolia was one among many indigenous regions becoming visible, as the depredations of Chinese conquest started to be evident.) This was echoed by a move from poetry like Artaud's, Euro-decadent, merely offensive to University administrators, to poetry and bioregional studies that bypass the premise that literature is a high art European enterprise, and that academic departments are the institutions charged with preserving it.

I want to mention one last defining journal of the period. *Alcheringa* appeared from 1970-1980, exactly spanning the seventies. It was co-edited by a poet who had done ethnographic fieldwork, Jerome Rothenberg, and an anthropologist, Dennis Tedlock, who was building on Charles Olson's attention to the breath in poetry to make unprecedented translations of oral narrative. In his 1978 Preface to *Finding the Center: Narrative Poetry of the Zuni Indians*, Tedlock directly brings the day's poetic explorations into the ethnographer's work.

> The reopening of possibilities in our own language goes hand in hand, or voice in voice, with *a new openness to the spoken words of other traditions*, especially those that spring from the same continent where we are now learning, however slowly, how to become natives. [My italics]

Alcheringa, like *Coyote's Journal*, published contemporary Native American poets, and like *Kuksu* used illustrative elements from pre-conquest American petroglyphs. Rothenberg & Tedlock were both working, in *Alcheringa*'s pages, towards what they termed "total translation." That is to say, an effort to translate "words, sounds & (to some extent) 'melody' into a visual field," (Rothenberg); as well as to incorporate on the visual page performance elements: dance, song, word-tone, ceremonial gesture, and audience participation. "Under the best circumstances," Rothenberg writes, "translation-for-meaning is no more than partial translation."

In all these publications the guiding effort seems to return poetry to its communal and ceremonial role. Returning the attention of poetry to voice, breath, body, to the body politic. This meant restoring it to a wider context: its ecology. I'm put in mind of the title of a Gary Snyder poem, "All the Animal Powers Return to Their Dancing Place." The work of that period pressed us all to acknowledge something: North American poetry is nothing without a full ecology of languages. Animal powers, plant powers, weather powers. It presumes a reckoning with the span of world verse, much of it oral, most of it non-Western, far from modern Anglo-European language habits and official verse culture.

Now: there are poets who do not translate. They remain beyond reproach; languages are tough to learn, and translation is accompanied by political and personal struggle. There are also poets who translate occasionally, with a sense that it keeps their hand in, or is a dignified aspect of "letters." In America most of these poet-translators venture to familiar European tongues & remain comfortably within the range of the last 200 years. But an alternate lineage in North American poetry always existed, which with no apology places translation, and an ecological sense of the planet's poetry, at the center of writing. Much of the translation for these poets (here is the ecology) is not from European languages alone: Chinese, Sanskrit, Mongolian, Mayan, Arabic. And the many hundreds of tongues, especially American Indian, that, existing perfectly well without writing systems, did not bother to develop a written literature. Navajo, Haida, Achomawi, Sioux, Chippewa. Interest in this range of literature—writing systems that stretch back millennia, and oral tradition (orature) that reaches far into the Paleolithic—runs counter to the isolating tendency of much American poetry, most college curricula, and nearly all the creative writing programs.

Ezra Pound late in *The Cantos* had growled, "It can't all be in one language."

If a single figure hovers over the project I'm describing—a totem or tutelary spirit—it is Jaime de Angulo, "the old coyote of Big Sur." De Angulo was a Paris-born Spaniard who came to North America's West Coast early in the twentieth century, a fine linguist, a determined anarchist, a suffragist, an army-trained psychologist, a wilderness homesteader. He developed a reputation as quite a wild man. He lived and worked with the Indians of California for decades, often funded by Franz Boas and The Committee on Research in Native American Languages, to learn and "write-up" the grammar, vocabulary, and stories of tribes he moved among. This was the "salvage ethnography" of the nineteen-twenties and thirties. De Angulo's many monographs, poems, stories, creation tales, and so forth revolve around his work with the Achomawi, Sierra Miwok, Pomo, Karok, Shasta, and other California peoples.[7] These things have, and continue to build, an ever-increasing influence on North American views of what "our" literature is.[8]

Though de Angulo died in 1950—the year he recorded his legendary eighty-eight-session magnum opus "Old Time Stories" (more regularly referred to by the 1953 book title *Indian Tales*) for KPFA community supported radio—you could say he really entered North American poetry in the seventies. His writings appear in each of the publications I've mentioned so far. I encountered him first in the pages of *America A Prophecy* ("Shaman Songs"), then in *Coyote's Journal, Kuksu,* and *Alcheringa. Alcheringa* even inserted a flappy three-minute vinyl disc of his KPFA storytelling in their first issue.

But it was Turtle Island Foundation's publication of the seven volume Jaime de Angulo Library in the early to mid-seventies, followed by 1978's *The Jaime de Angulo Reader,* that got his work out to people who couldn't tune in Pacifica Radio's yearly re-broadcasts of the old "Indian Tales" tapes.

The Turtle Island books are gorgeous: pocket-size hard-bound editions, designed by either Clifford Burke or Graham MacIntosh, two of the era's fine hand-printers and influential book designers. The print-runs were 1000 to 1500 copies a volume, but impact can't be calculated in numbers. While many became treasures on a poet's bookshelf, others circulated on backcountry trips, and went readily hand to hand among friends. It is fortunate the publisher bound them in cloth; most copies I've seen on peoples' bookshelves are powerfully worn by repeated reading.

If you don't live in Northern California, from Big Sur to Berkeley, or out to the Sierra Nevada, or north to Arcata on the coast, it might be hard to imagine the grip de Angulo has on the imagination of people who live a bit outside the mainstream. I was in Arcata a few summers ago and stopped into the local used bookstore, which has a fine section on Native American studies. I was looking for books that might help with a project on de Angulo. I picked off the shelf a book I hadn't seen before, an anthology of California Indian literature,[9] which turned out to have William Ralganal Benson's "Pomo Creation Myth" in the translation he did with de Angulo. I'd hardly opened the cover when behind me a soft voice said, "That's a fine book."

A man in plaid shirt, gray ponytail, beard, and work boots stood thoughtfully looking at me through wire rim glasses. I wondered would he be a professor at Humboldt State University just up the hill, which houses a sizeable Native American studies department. "Do you teach with it?" "No, I just know the book. It's excellent." That could have been the end of the conversation, but I tried a hunch. "I was looking for something on Jaime de Angulo." He searched my eyes for a long moment, then replied with ceremonial gravity. "I married my wife because she was reading Jaime de Angulo."

•

Tradition lies buried in the land, and geography, like poetry, is an essential mode of attention.
Jerome Rothenberg

Time now, with those various publications in mind, to bring forward a profile of poets who write from familiarity with the types of influence I've tried to sketch. As I said at the opening of this talk, they seem a school that is not a school, more a series of figures in a shared ecology. I could name a lot of poets, and could place many more in the alleys or ravines, or back along the fences, but will simply note that the Pacific coast is a stronghold. So is the Southwest. So is New England. All three areas have a strong vernacular culture, and just as important, large undeveloped territories (wilderness), and a good-size heritage of aboriginal lore. I have no idea how interested any of the poets are in being thought of as a school or a defined movement so I won't compile any extensive lists. I'll write down some notable tendencies though.

—*Live or have lived largely in non-urban locations*[10]

—*Prefer low impact, low consumption lifestyle; use of local resources: firewood, gardens, hunting, fishing*

—*Attentive to their own (& other's) watersheds*

—*Possess authentic wilderness skills & outdoor capabilities*

—*An ethos of work with manual tools*

—*An ethos & a poetics that take into account the land; hence nature literate: plant lore; animal lore; star lore; land stewardship*

—*Often learned in fields other than poetry; botany, ecology, anthropology, linguistics, &c; few make their living at academic work however: amateur*

—*As or more attuned to Asian or archaic poetics than to European, a sizable number knowing one or more Asian or non-European language and translating the poetry*

—*For politics: loyal to bioregional concerns; decentralized decision-making; representational democracy; a strong dose of anarchist thought; a sometimes redneck anti-authoritarian skepticism*

The poetry—

—*Projectivist tendencies*

—*Organic form preferred to regularized metrics and stanzas*

—*Belief in poetry as communal, hence occasional poems and friendship poems, love poems, protest poetry, &c.*

—*Concrete elements & sound poetry, hence a concern with the material base of language*

— *"Hand-made" publications: the poets & their friends skilled in*
   book design, woodblock or linoleum prints, letterpress printing,
   desktop, and samizdat
—*Ethnopoetics & aboriginal lore*

A network of cottage industry (small press) publishing has emerged, and forms loose Post Coyote links.[11] Bob and Susan Arnold's Longhouse has been issuing hand-made items since the early seventies. Theirs would be one exemplary model, one that could stand for all the others. Bob's stonework, hauling, carpentry, and woodcutting, Susan's secretary work & computer skills, create the economic base. Their preferred item is what I call a "chaplet," a little fold-out of a few poems, tucked into stiff wrappers—"Origami for your pocket" (JB Bryan). One of their press statements captures the spirit: "Longhouse takes on no grants, funding or subscription. Rather has been self-supported through the good heart of the poets and readers of the journal."

Outfits that keep both bioregion and *Internationale* in sight, that remain largely free of government funding, and publish in the post coyote vein, include La Alameda Press, Empty Bowl, Tangram, Exiled-in-America, White Pine, Tooth of Time, *Malpaís Review*, Voices from the American Land, and to some extent Jack Shoemaker's Counterpoint Press, which has survived several deaths and rebirths, changing its name each time. Counterpoint has made reliable translations from East Asia, both poetry and Buddhist texts, one of its cornerstones. It also publishes two singular poets who stand as spokespersons for conservation and agricultural reform, Gary Snyder and Wendell Berry. Meanwhile, links to urban-based, experimental poets come through journals such as Hoa Nguyen and Dale Smith's now defunct *Skanky Possum* with its hand-colored covers, Jonathan Skinner's exemplary *Ecopoetics*, and the late Sylvester Pollet's aptly named *backwoods broadsides*. Many similar enterprises continue to appear. The huge number of small, do it yourself publications is one of North American poetry's most vital aspects: "The small press is the natural habitat of the poem."

If you want to go a bit deeper, it's worth calling up the website for *Coyote's Journal*. Take a look at their covers, and the list of books they've published over the years. You can still find copies of the out-of-print *America A Prophecy* in the stacks of our remaining independent used bookshops (this spring, 2013, it has come back into print after a long time away). And there is Bob Arnold's on-line annotated bibliography of Longhouse titles, stretching from 1971 to the present, which maintains close links to European concrete poets as well as to contemporary Asian American poets and a range of translation that makes Green River, Vermont, seem as worldly and far hipper than the United Nations.

One Longhouse foldout chapbook was titled *Out There*, a poem written when I heard that poet Bill Everson had died. Bill stands as one of the cardinal San Francisco Renaissance figures: fierce poet with an eye for wilderness; radical pacifist who'd been shipped to an internment camp for resisting conscription into the armed forces during World War II. Everson turned himself into a meticulous, self-trained letterpress printer & bookmaker, and for twenty years lived as a monk in the Dominican order. During the nineteen-seventies, living in a cottage in the woods north of Santa Cruz, he became a spokesperson for ecological wisdom, turning to St. Francis to recover a little-known line of conservation & ecological sanity in the Catholic Church.

During the late seventies I'd worked on a letterpress book with Everson at Santa Cruz's Lime Kiln Press, *Blame It On the Jet Stream*. Bill had delivered the poem—its thundering, prophetic lines and stark imagery an effort to come to terms with violence in nature & in the local community—as a graduation address in 1973. Due to Bill's ecology studies, handcraft approach to bookmaking, anarchist-pacifist commitment, & rural lifestyle, his writings stand as those of a Post Coyote culture hero. In homage to the "mountain man" culture of the Western states (plus deeper homage to the animal powers), Bill had shed his Dominican habit for buckskin vest, bear-claw necklace, and rattlesnake hatband. Here, in this bibliographic entry for *Out There*, it is Bob Arnold's tone I want to point out. It feels personable, hand-made, done "through the good

BLAME IT ON THE JET STREAM!

By William Everson

Ode: The First Commencement, June 17, 1973
Kresge College, The University of California at Santa Cruz

Foreword by the Author: Woodcut by Dennis Marks

The Lime Kiln Press: 1978

heart of the poets" as he says. He's unafraid to note quirky detail, because all is relevant to what goes into making a book.

> Andrew probably appeared after Cid Corman mentioned my name
> and press. He's a very curious devil, regardless. Has had his hand in
> a long span of poetry, reaching back to Sanskrit translations (some
> of his finest work), running awhile with small press editing and
> publishing, yeoman bookshop work in California, sterling personal
> essays, and many years staffed at the Naropa Institute with the
> children of Albion. He's a maker and a doer. Andrew's walked many
> times into our yard from a long distance off bringing parts of his
> family with him for a visit. The spiritual father William Everson
> was but one of his friends.

A few final thoughts, spurred by musing on Jaime de Angulo's ethnographic writings. These have to do with the contradictory ways the figure of coyote shows up in stories, hence germinal to my own foolish effort to locate a school that is not a school, and then to call this non-existent aggregate of poets by name: Post Coyote.

"Child, there are so many Coyotes," writes de Angulo, "... wise Coyotes, foolish Coyotes ... that's just the way people are. There have been all kinds of Coyotes ever since the world began."[12]

In Western American folklore—among indigenous peoples of the Plains, the Southwest, and California, as well as among Anglo and Spanish settlers—two seemingly contradictory Coyote figures show up. The first Coyote is a character who scrambles the qualities of the fool with those of a clever magician; in de Angulo's words, "always getting into trouble, always getting out of it by the measure of his own cleverness." Put this figure into poetry terms and he could be Coyote Dada, the interloper who rummages around the back allies of North American cities. A dumpster diver, he is prototype or patron of those artists who perform outrageous acts—acts that mock and deconstruct stuffy unexamined notions about art. Every age has its impasses. To get through them the petrified ideas need to be broken apart, so this I guess is Coyote Dada's task. It is what the urban avant-garde has proved so good at.

By contrast another Coyote peoples the folklore, not generally brash and foolish, but more a creator figure. He is the innovator: in Ezra Pound's term, a founder, the poet who makes something new. This one's the culture hero, the inventor, the woman or man who has sunk deep into the needs of the contemporary, and won through to a new perspective: Coyote Pulitzer. Such an artist brings forth work that moves everyone towards the future. My sense is that fewer of these creator figures arise than of that other, the foolish-clever Coyote breed that causes havoc with obsolete ideas. But we need them both.

And then, because "there have been all kinds of Coyotes since the world began," a third sort of Coyote wanders around inside the lore. This is Coyote Old Man, the sage, inscrutable doctor. Nobody knows where he came from or how long he's been around. All anyone knows is that this Coyote is very old indeed—grandfather or grandmother of everybody, the one who comes up with a solution when things get really tough. I'd say this one's the salt dog who carries forward all manner of bits and pieces of the past; when necessary this Coyote pulls something from the little buckskin sack around his or her neck, and with what nobody else thought to save, resolves the crisis of the moment. He or she is the culture bearer, holder of old poems, translator of early traditions, a walking anthology. This Coyote interprets prosody, metrics, poetic form, is a collector of lyrics, reader of signs. The troubador who never goes away.

These three Coyote figures do not represent separate people, of course—not in our own mixed up world. I think they embody three types of work poets do. All who write in the post Coyote tradition house a little bit of each inside themselves. The fool who tries impossible things and busts apart the assumptions of the old order. The creator who energetically builds something new. The sage priest who carries the best of the past in a little buckskin pouch at his or her neck, who brings it forth judiciously, right when everybody's at a loss as to where, exactly, to go.

1. I believe first reports of coyote on the East Coast came in the mid to late 1970s.

2. Clayton Eshleman writes: "I last visited the (N.O.) Brown's in 1990. We had dinner at their house. That evening at least, Brown was obsessed with the 1960s. He told me that his discovery of the poetry of Robert Duncan had made the writing of *Love's Body* possible. I said I thought it was William Blake that led to the breakdown of rational procedure in that book. No, it was Duncan, he insisted, then saying: And I couldn't figure out how to get more of him into the book." *Archaic Design*, p. 204. See also Dale Pendell, *Walking with Nobby: Conversations with Norman O. Brown*, for Brown's relationship with M.C. Richards.

3. *Kuksu: Journal of Backcountry Writing, no. 4*, "Work." Pendell says (personal correspondence, 2008): "Original name of Kuksu was Kyoi, a Sinkyone creator figure from Humboldt County, where the first two issues came out. I changed it to Kuksu when I moved to the Sierras—as a culture figure known to both the Coast Range and the Sierra."

4. Henry Kissinger's "secret visit" to mainland China occurred July 8-11, 1971. In February, 1972, President Richard Nixon visited China, & met with Mao Zedong. With "the Shanghai Communiqué" of February 28 Nixon reestablished formal ties between the U.S.A. and China. Friends I knew in college at the time received the benefit of money suddenly poured into East Asian studies—from the State Department, business interests, and so forth. Several friends were approached by the CIA and offered positions. For many years, Western students in the People's Republic of China were heavily restricted as to where they could go, and Taiwan remained a more genial option for poets. But it was the reawakened sense of China's

importance, and the influx of funding, that gave a practical base to American poets hoping to learn the language.

5. The town of Port Townsend alone has had three prolific Chinese translators, Sam Hamill, Mike O'Connor, and Red Pine. Its local press, Copper Canyon, has published Asian translations from Caroline Kizer, Arthur Sze, W.S. Merwin, Kenneth Rexroth, and dozens of others. See in particular Copper Canyon's title, edited by Frank Stewart, *The Poem Behind the Poem: Translating Asian Poetry*.

6. Tartarus in Greek myth lies lower than Hades. It is reserved for those who make war on the gods. If an anvil takes nine days to fall from Heaven to Earth, it takes another nine days to reach the realm of Tartarus (Hesiod). The word is cognate to tortoise, (Portugese: tartaruga). In some Native American & many Asian cosmologies, when you get all the way down it is a turtle that upholds the earth: "Turtle Island, the old-new name for this continent" (Gary Snyder). Snyder's collection of poetry *Turtle Island*, his effort to bring the revolution to the back country, received the Pulitzer Prize in 1974.

7. The scholarly accounts of de Angulo say he did field work, and subsequently "wrote up" the grammars of twenty-six Amerindian and native Mexican languages. His book *Indian Tales*, and the KPFA radio broadcasts of 1950, include translations from quite a few languages of Northern California—languages often as different as Chinese is from Sanskrit. See his bibliography in *Jaime in Taos* (City Lights), compiled by Wendy Leeds-Hurvitz.

8. See p. 157, "The Songs of Jaime de Angulo," for a closer look at this material.

9. *Surviving through the Days: A California Indian Reader*, edited by Herbert Luthin.

10. Jennifer Moxley asks whether rural economics, and the manual labor required in back woods child rearing (such as washing diapers by hand) make this "school" masculinist, male dominated. That is worth exploring, though I can think of many women poets I would cluster in or near the Post Coyote camp—a brief list would include Joanne Kyger, Barbara Moraff, Renée Gregorio, Hoa Nguyen. Not all live in remote rural communities, but they share a language of the "international archaic." I also wonder if the shifting fortunes of work such as midwifery, herb-craft, and other healing arts—due to state laws, AMA politics, insurance company policies, &c— have had a depressing effect on the economic lives of scholarly rural women.

About the labor involved in child rearing Hoa Nguyen writes me: " . . . toilet learning practices in non Western parts of the globe do not include diapering. Many parents use what is called 'elimination communication' here [in the U.S.A.]. Do you remember seeing diapering during your early travels in India? In China they still dress toddlers in pants that are open at the seam and up the back so the child can quickly squat . . . I was EC'd in Vietnam. When I arrived to the US at 18 months my words were for needing to urinate or defecate (sounding something like EEN and OON but with diphthong tones). I wasn't in a diaper.

"We did EC with Waylon starting as a newborn . . . so anyway, I'm not sure of the connection between living in rural versus urban areas, re: labor and diapering. Unless by rural, Jennifer means they are poor with no means or access to a washing machine. Cloth diapering is not arduous (in my experience) and cheaper than the plastic disposables. And hanging diapers on a clothesline is hardly a time consuming task (or tossing in the dryer). In my mind, labor and resources are enmeshed. Time (labor) is a resource (you can monetize). If by using cloth you save money, you save your labor, too."

11. "The law of metamorphosis": *Coyote's Journal* emerges out of a suppressed issue of the *Northwest Review*. *Kyoi* shifts locale and adopts another culture hero for its name, *Kuksu*. *Alcheringa* condenses into *New Wilderness Newsletter*. Longhouse & *Origin* start to publish hand-in-hand & regularly exchange authors. The handmade ethos & modest dimension of many publications—letterpress, or small "chaplet" constructed at home, book covers sometimes silk-screened or inventively hand-colored—forefront the material base of publication.

12. From Jaime de Angulo, *Shabegok*, one of the Turtle Island Press volumes (1976). The book's a somewhat disordered collection of material that never made it into the heavily cut, posthumous *Indian Tales*.

Books for the Game Drive Walls

"One of the penalties of an ecological education," wrote Aldo Leopold, "is that one lives alone in a world of wounds. Much of the damage inflicted on the land is quite invisible to laymen." Thanks to a lucky strike that occurred several years ago, I began to flip this statement over, and to consider how one of the benefits of a bit of archaeological inquiry and ecological education is that these offer entry to a world of good medicine. Using Leopold's phrasing, you enter a world invisible to laymen; but you don't need to go it alone.

The strike took place in May 2008, when a cache of prehistoric tools came to light in Boulder, Colorado. The cache-site lies only five minutes by automobile from Naropa University's campus (where I teach), in the yard of a comfortable home tucked up where elegant neighborhoods have encroached on the Ponderosa-pine-covered foothills. The Mahaffey Cache is named for the Boulder resident and landowner whose landscape gardener's spade first sparked against the stone tools. Had the planned layout of Mahaffey's garden-in-progress been a bit different, the cache may never have come to light. In a cavity slightly larger than a shoebox lay eighty-three or eighty-four blades, scrapers, and spear points, chipped out of ergonomically shaped local stone.

On the hand-knapped tools lab scientists found 'protein residue' of the North American horse and camel—two creatures that vanished for still-uncertain reasons about 10,000 years ago, near the end of the last Ice Age. The tools also yielded residue of the American short-nosed bear, also long vanished—a creature twice the size of a grizzly and capable of running sixty miles per hour. (Hard to imagine taking—with a stone-tipped weapon—a predator that could chase down your Subaru & peel it open.) The Boulder cache was evidently somebody's, more likely some band's, butcher kit.

Likely the tools' holders stashed it at a strategic point on an annual migration route, near a campsite alongside a stream now buried by pavement, and for reasons invisible to us never returned.

Ongoing interest in the cache—& its portal into Deep Time—prompted me to deepen my own explorations into the "what-went-here-before," and to muse on the relevance of archaic tools for contemporary poetry. I turned to a careful rereading of George C. Frison's 2004 book, *Survival by Hunting: Prehistoric Human Predators and Animal Prey*. Frison is an expert on Paleoindian kill sites; his book was written soberly and with great care. It is worth reading with equal care and sobriety. He grew up on a ranch in Wyoming, hunted from the time his family entrusted him with a rifle, spent years among game animals, predators, ranching culture, and has observed the historical shifts in hunting that occurred over the years. An early chapter, "The Education of a Hunter," makes good reading to understand the ethos of hunting as he found it on the High Plains, at a time and in a region where hunting was a substantial and highly regarded skill of subsistence, particularly in the years around the Great Depression.

After World War II, with growth in the American population, a surge in the American economy, and the introduction of high power rifles, hunting altered. Frison discusses the changes—in particular his own growing unease with trophy hunting, which had largely replaced survival, and his eventual decision to leave his job as a hunting guide and turn towards archaeology as a profession. He had always been intrigued by prehistoric sites on the Wyoming plains, and on findings that threw light on old-time hunting. His contribution is to bring a hunter's skilled eye and detailed knowledge of animal behavior into the academic discipline. His accounts of Paleoindian kill sites—for bison, pronghorn, mountain sheep, and for extinct mammals such as the mastadon—are scrupulous. So are his accounts of stone butcher tools from Clovis culture on. He has replicated the tools (imagine chipping your own butcher's kit), and used them on the hides of elephant, bison, and elk, to understand how the Paleolithic toolkit functioned, how precisely an edge must be flaked, how quickly the tools dull or the spearhead shatters.

Since the large kill sites in prehistoric and historic times often used human-constructed walls or corrals to funnel or contain the quarry, Frison's descriptions of these, along with a spare use of photos, are crucial information about the era before our own. I recently hiked with botanist friend Tim Hogan into the Indian Peaks Wilderness in search of Paleoindian game drive walls we'd heard of. We used a book—now hard to procure—*This Land of Shining Mountains*, edited by E. Steve Cassels. Its several chapters detail a set of drive walls, each excavated by a different archaeologist, in the Indian Peaks: at Devil's Thumb Pass, up the Fourth of July Valley, in the Woodland drainage, and on the flanks of Sawtooth. On the southern slope of the saddle above Betty and Bob Lakes—about a six mile hike in—with shouts & clapping hands Tim and I found the wall we'd gone in search of, using a map and aerial photos from Cassels' book. The wall we examined was used—possibly 1650 years ago, and it may have been built on the ruins of older walls—to corner migrating elk, at an elevation of about 11,800', likely during the autumn southward journey of the herds.

Stand above the wall, on a sizeable boulder, and watch the wall drop down the slope below. It veers towards some bad footing. Notice pillow-size slabs leaning against support rocks; study the hogback appearance of bristling granite; carefully turn one hand-placed rock (I'm not sure if this is legal at an archaeological site supervised by the Forest Service) to see no lichen on its down side (indicating it has sat a long time in its current position).

If you've read Frison's book you will immediately conjure more than a wall. Likely the hunters erected poles or staffs of wood. Flapping hides or feathers, maybe painted skins, strands of beads, rattling deer hooves, or bundles of vegetable matter, would have added height & drama to the walls. Wind flapping the items madly in ghostly mist. A fringed rawhide tunic leaping out of the clouds. The panicked animals would race down-slope onto boulder fields that hung them up, or into fresh snowfields where waiting spearmen could take the slowed quarry.

Most curious are a number of circular "blinds"—rock lined shallow pits, ten or fifteen feet in diameter, their walls slightly built up by hand-placed rock. In them hunters may have concealed themselves under skins. At the walls and blinds above Devil's Thumb, we talked of sleeping in these pits. Following Frison's reading of Northern Plains kill sites, might some have been "shaman huts"? It seems a bit risky without knowing their early use, to entrust these pits with your dreams, here at 12,125' elevation.

> Without known exception, ceremonial activity accompanied ethnographic accounts of communal bison hunting, and the structure alongside the Ruby site corral can only be interpreted in this same context. David Mandelbaum claimed that the building of a Cree pound was supervised by a shaman who, when the trap was in operation, placed his tipi by the entrance, where he invoked spirit helpers to ensure success. (p. 92)

> It is possible (though this suggestion is purely speculative) that as a part of the labor-intensive construction of the ramp at the Muddy Creek corral, a space for the shaman was left beneath it and between the posts holding it up. *There he could perform his rituals of calling in the animals.* (p. 94) [My italics.]

> At the Jones-Miller site of Hell Gap age [10,000 BP] . . . a posthole with several objects, likely to have been ceremonial, around its base and a large hearth nearby with associated patches of yellow and red ochre suggested ritual activity. The hole may have contained *a "medicine post," which the shaman climbed to conduct ritual activities before and during the killing of the animals.* (p. 96-7) [My italics.]

> Remains of small wood and stone structures incorporated into drive lines that do not appear to affect the traps' functional utility are believed to have been associated with a shaman . . . (p. 158)

[T]he preservation of parts of a bison corral and an associated religious structure, a shaman's structure incorporated into the drive line of a sheep trap, a circle of bison skulls in a bone bed, deer skulls with antlers attached set in a pattern around another skull placed on top of a rock cairn, and the like—provide rare glimpses of ritual observances in the past and remind us to allow for their presence. (pp. 226-7)

Notice Frison's extreme reserve regarding what he calls ritual activity. He cites historic accounts of Native hunting for parallels, but with the exception of a few examples from his own encounters with the 'superstitious behavior' of modern hunters, never attempts to speculate on what any of it might mean.

As a poet, I stay on the lookout for material that bears on origins of poetic technique, especially of the more innovative sort: ritual distortion of words, taboo word replacement, mnemonic rhythmic structure, compressed syntax, nonsensical phonemes. Native American song traditions—which include hunting songs—are full of these techniques, helpful instruction for those who know that 'the meaning exceeds the words' in poetry. One often hopes to catch a piece of song—if not off the sharp winds creasing the Continental Divide then from the early literature of North America. Wouldn't Frison's "calling in [of] the animals" likely incorporate song? But his book is not intended to look into this.

For which reason I am enormously grateful to Canadian poet Robert Bringhurst's writings on Native American oral literature, his translations in particular of the Haida 'mythtellers' Ghandl and Skaay. Counterpoint Press brought out Bringhurst's *The Tree of Meaning: Language, Mind and Ecology*, in 2008. Its opening essay, "The Polyhistorical Mind," speaks of Canadian literature, but could serve as well for any of us other North Americans:

A literary map of this country would be first of all a map of languages, several layers deep. On the base layers, there would be no sign of English and French. At least sixty-five, perhaps as many as eighty, different languages, of at least ten different major language families, were spoken in this country when Jacques Carrier arrived. Each of them had a history and a literature. It is with them, or what remains of them, that the study of Canadian literature must start.

Why might we consider learning something about these literatures, which were far more abundant in what is today called the United States? (Estimates of 600 languages at the time of contact with European settlers; a current count of sixty-two language *families*.) Partly it is that "they are the legacy, after all, of people who knew how to live in this land for thousands of years without wrecking it." Bringhurst insists— once you begin to explore, it seems obvious—that a study of literature, American, Canadian, or Mexican, starts at these base layers. His own finest encounter is in a trilogy of books devoted to the oral tales of the Haida. Of these, *A Story as Sharp as a Knife* (1999), is the "commentary" around the two other volumes, which are the mythtelling or epic poems of two Haida masters, who he regards as our equivalents of Homer. The books are *Nine Visits to the Myth World* by Ghandl, and Skaay's *Being in Being*, which includes the wildly surrealist epic "Raven Traveling," full of animal transformations, feats of magical adventure, trickery, humor. All of it originating in a hunting culture that was relatively intact until the nineteenth century.

Then, when he had flown a while longer,
something brightened to the north.
It caught his eye, they say.
And then he flew right up against it.

He pushed his mind through
and pulled his body after.

There were five villages strung out in a line...

Yet *Story*, at 527 pages, is not simply commentary. If a contemporary, non-Haida reader—of European, African, or Asian heritage—feels a bit squeamish adopting "Raven Traveling" as one's own epic, embedded as it is in a culture of sea-hunting people, this third volume of Bringhurst's trilogy feels to be 'a poem including history,' specifically our own. It is the finest account I've read of the Boasian project in "salvage ethnography." Its cast of characters radiates out from the ethnographer John Swanton, who had appeared fresh out of graduate school on Haida Gwaii (today's Queen Charlotte Islands) in 1900, and began work in the village of Skidegate. Franz Boas, Alfred Kroeber, Ruth Benedict, Elsie Clew Parsons, and numerous other ethnographers, translators, and linguists appear; also scavengers, thieves, colonists. The focus remains with the Haida though. Gumsiiwa's poem:

When she kept saying the same thing,
the one who was lying by the fire said,
"Tell me, why do you keep talking?"

"Well, sir, I'm not just talking to my own ears.
The spirit-beings tell me that they have no place to live.
That's the reason I keep talking."

There are stories of contact, conquest, disease; songs and tales; & natural history, as when Bringhurst speaks of the migratory sea life (fish, shellfish, sea mammals) that pass in front of the ocean-facing Haida villages as "an edible calendar," a phrase pried from the book as you might an oyster from its shell.

Bringhurst's title comes from a Haida saying, "the world is as sharp as a knife." *Tlgaay higha ttlabju' waaga.* More accurately, "the world is sharp as a woodcutter's blade (or woodcutter's wedge) standing straight up." Ghandl and Skaay don't just reiterate old tellings; they use their art to encounter the knife-edge sharp world out ahead, and use that world to keep the edge on their stories.

The West Coast had an extraordinary richness of languages prior to the appearance of European settlers. It still does, though painfully reduced and redistributed. Look at any map of Native languages (such as the good *Native Languages and Language Families of North America*, compiled by Ives Goddard). You'll see that language families like Algic, Nadene (which includes Navajo), and Siouan-Catawba cover vast territories, hundreds of thousands of square miles. By contrast the narrow Left Coast, between the ocean and the Sierra Nevada's east slope, from about contemporary San Diego north to Haida Gwai, is a patchwork of dozens of linguistic families, the tongues as different from each other as Greek from Nahuatl, Hebrew from Basque. What produced such extraordinary diversity? Whatever the reason, the richness remains the "base layer" necessary to understanding such later poetry episodes as the S.F. Renaissance, or the profusion of current California poetry written, often multilingually, in Spanish, Chinese, Phillipino, as well as English, Karok, & Japanese.

For California, the good Deep Time collection is Herbert Luthin's *Surviving Through the Days: A California Indian Reader.* This is the great ghost gallery of remarkable story-tellers: William Ralganal Benson, Sally Noble, Ishi, Mabel McKay, Grace McKibbon. The rogue's gallery of anthropologists, sometimes divided into collectors, translators, transcribers, or commentators: Alfred Kroeber, Edward Sapir, J.P. Harrington, Dorothy Demetracopoulou, Leanne Hinton. And Jaime de Angulo.

If you have been frustrated that all seven volumes of the Jaime de Angulo Library (Turtle Island Press, 1970s), designed and printed by Clifford Burke, are long unavailable, with Luthin's volume you can at least get the Pomo creation tale written down by Benson and de Angulo. (This text was the final volume in the de Angulo Library, *How the World Was Made.*) It tells how the Kuksu and the Marumda, using their thoughts and their tobacco—& in some recitations their songs—made and destroyed the world until with the fifth formation they got it pretty good. Luthin, in his introductory essay to Benson and de Angulo, cites a passage from de Angulo's book *Indian Tales*.

> "That was surely a frightening-looking figure," Killeli said. "Is the Kuksu a killer, like the Giants and the Imps over in my country?"
>
> "Oh, of course not," Old Man Coyote said. "Why should he hurt anybody? The Kuksu doesn't care about people, one way or another. The Kuksu's no killer."
>
> "But, Grandfather, doesn't the Kuksu take care of the world?" Tsimmu asked.
>
> "No, Child. The world pretty much takes care of itself."

Luthin's accompanying essays (some at the front, others at the rear of the book) are worth reading closely. He gives the best, terse account I have seen of the contributions made by Dennis Tedlock and Dell Hymes to Ethnopoetic translation. Tedlock of course drew on Charles Olson's "Projective Verse," to locate a voice-based notation of oral literature. Working with Zuni story-tellers, Tedlock utilized the range of the typewriter to 'score' on the page: loudness of voice, emphasis or saliency, pauses, and other vocal techniques, including formal or informal audience response. Dell Hymes devised another method of scoring, using syntax, grammar, narrative phrasing, key words, and those sort of linguistic criteria to develop 'lines' and 'stanzas'. Luthin observes that most translators of Native American material these days mix the methods, as well as using other techniques suggested by the specific language they're working.

A dream song from the Wintu, sung by Jennie Curl in 1930 (Dorothy Demetracopoulou, collector and translator):

Of course,
If I went to Stillwater
I might choke on a grasshopper leg.

Yeah, but—
If I went to the Upper Sacramento
I might choke on the bone of a fawn . . .

This, if you didn't catch it, is a song of derision (*nini*), taken from a hunting culture. One girl, two men—read through the sarcasm to see which is the better provider.

In March or April, 2009, the Scottish poet Eck Finlay wrote asking if I'd compose a mountain poem in about ten lines, for one of his British mountain sky-line poetry projects. I thought of the Mahaffey Cache, recently surfaced in my home town, as a find that had altered our sense of mountains and how humans dwell in them. The resulting stanza became the opening of my sequence "From the ARAPAHO SONGBOOK." A good (if technical) book, which I draw on quite a bit as the sequence proceeds, contains tales from this mountain-plains bioregion where I live and work: *Hinóno'éínoo3ítoono: Arapaho Historical Traditions, told by Paul Moss* (2005). Moss's stories are translated by Andrew Cowell, a linguist at the University of Colorado, along with Alonzo Moss, Sr., a native speaker from the Wind River Reservation.

The translators have scored the collection's narratives into poetry-strophes using several criteria—narrative phrasing, length of pauses, and especially the presence of the word *Wohéí*, something like, "okay, now, then, it happened that" signaling a change in location, a new character, a shift in perspective. The book is bilingual; paired with their grammar *The Arapaho Language* (2008) it provides a sound basis for study of Arapaho, an Algonkian tongue. (Edward Sapir: "Single Algonkian words are like tiny Imagist poems.")

44

I should confess that after thirty-plus years working with Sanskrit, Arapaho defeats me. Yet when I examine its division of the world into two 'genders', animate and inanimate, or comb through the obviative case (a sort of fourth person, lacking a clear occurrence in English) I feel my heart race. The stories too are exhilarating. Particularly when you get enough Arapaho under your belt to sound out the original, and switch back & forth with English. That a coyote possessed of medicine power—in the opening tale—can use the obviative without faltering, spurs me to harder study.

Andrew Cowell, one of the authors of these studies, I have gotten to know. Hiked with him to the Divide, talking Ethnopoetics, plant lore, bear mythology. We have eaten mountain blueberries (tiny as a pin head in drought years), straw huckleberries, and buffalo-berry. His and Mr. Moss's books have been at my side for the past couple of years: 'base layer' to the Rocky Mountain and High Plains region where home & job are. Novice that I am, I see how well Arapaho held the plants, animals, land forms, and weather patterns, and how awkwardly suited such recent arrivals are as English, Spanish, or taxonomic Latin.

Cowell turned me on to an older title, *Giving Voice to Bear*, by David Rockwell—a compendium of North American Indian stories, rites, and the like, regarding *Ursus arctos* and *Ursus americanus*—grizzly and black bears. This lore may not mean much if you live in Miami, but it's significant on terrain where "the bear went over the mountain" feels as deep in your blood as "born under a bad sign." Terrain where any October excursion into the hills might result in a bear encounter. After all, these creatures feed on a diet close to our own, and were nearby presences to those who built the game drive walls. They (we) once shared berry patches, trout in the creeks, venison, and now and then (if you follow the stories), a husband or wife.

In Rockwell's book you find Maria Johns, the Tagish storyteller, recounting a story that has received increased attention through the years, "the woman who married a bear." A somewhat different version occurs, called "The Bear Girl," in Luthin's California anthology. In California the storyteller is Sally Noble, and the translator Katherine Turner who writes: "The line breaks are an attempt to suggest the controlled, rhythmic pace of delivery that seems implicit in the language of the original."

> Her mother hired a good Indian doctor to ask
> what was the matter with the girl.
> She was not like our people.
> She was not like our flesh.
> She was not a person.
> She was not a human woman.
> She was going to turn out to be a bear.
> That's what the matter was.

Sally Noble's tale I want to single out for a minute. It is notable for the time in which the tireless, amateur ethnographer J.P. Harrington recorded it by hand, in a phonetic script (used when the original tongue has no writing system). "The Bear Girl" is the last tale told in the Chimariko language; Sally Noble was the last speaker of the tongue. "She spoke in English at first, then in both Chimariko and English, and, finally, in Chimariko with an occasional English word or phrase," wrote Harrington. She told her tale at the end of 1921 in a series of sessions (Harrington's Chimariko notebooks contain thousands of pages). As a bit of synchronicity, this was precisely when T.S. Eliot was readying *The Waste Land and Other Poems* for publication. Harrington went home to compile his notebooks, intending to return the following year and continue work with Sally. But Sally Noble died in February 1922, the month Eliot's book appeared in London.

"The Waste Land" altered the visible landscape of Modernism. The invisible landscape was changing at the same time. As Leopold wrote, "Much of the damage inflicted on the land is invisible to laymen."

BIBLIOGRAPHY

Bringhurst, Robert. *A Story as Sharp as a Knife: The Classical Haida Mythtellers and Their World.* University of Nebraska: Lincoln, 1999.

————. *The Tree of Meaning: Language, Mind and Ecology.* Counterpoint Press: Berkeley, 2008.

Cowell, Andrew with Alonzo Moss, Sr. *The Arapaho Language.* University Press of Colorado: Boulder, 2005

Frison, George C. *Survival by Hunting: Prehistoric Human Predators and Animal Prey.* University of California: Berkeley, 2004.

Goddard, Ives. *Native Languages and Language Families of North America.* (Map.) University of Nebraska Press: Lincoln, 1999.

Luthin, Herbert. *Surviving Through the Days: A California Indian Reader.* University of California: Berkeley, 2002.

Moss, Paul. *Hinóno'éínoo3ítoono: Arapaho Historical Traditions.* Edited, translated, and with a glossary by Andrew Cowell and Alonzo Moss, Sr. The University of Manitoba Press: Winnipeg, 2005.

Rockwell, David. *Giving Voice to Bear: North American Indian Myths, Rituals, and Images of the Bear.* Roberts Rinehart Publishers: Niwot, Colorado, 1999.

Drawing/collages of the proposed "sculpture" by Christo

OVER THE RIVER AGAIN

I

THE *New York Times* OBITUARY FOR LUNA B. LEOPOLD (MARCH 20, 2006) reminds me how little we know about rivers. Luna was the son of Aldo Leopold, whose *Sand County Almanac* and land management essays are basic eco-consciousness documents, and the first to articulate a land ethic that has come to appear a necessity and not merely a compelling idea. A fine scientist in his own right, Luna edited his father's journals for publication, and devoted his professional studies to America's river systems. "We in the United States have acquiesced to the destruction and degradation of our rivers, in part because we have insufficient knowledge of the characteristics of rivers and the effects of our actions that alter their form and process." That's on the first page of *A View of the River,* issued in paperback shortly before Luna's death.

What Leopold did best was figure ways to measure characteristics no one had ever established: river depth, water velocity, shapes of channels, sediments; the seemingly whimsical layout of rocks, how they got where they are, and what their effects on currents are; how currents carry particles down riverbeds. Working with the U.S. Geological Survey for ten years he pioneered the study of rivers in their terrain. He angled his eye to learn about slopes, hills, rock gradient, floodplains, stream banks, and the geology that underlies river systems.

Rivers take shape and shape their landscapes by meandering, and Leopold notes that the meander is "the pattern most prevalent in nature." That's why, I suppose, the map of a watershed looks like the veins in a leaf or a hand. As the Oglala Sioux medicine man Black Elk told the poet John Neihardt in a similar context, "They have the same religion we do."

Earth is the only planet we know of with a hydrologic or water cycle. So far it is the only planet we know of with biological life. Water evaporates from oceans into the air, moves with the wind, drops on the land as rain or snow, sinks into the soil, evaporates, and transpires from plants. About a third of what hits land drains through the continents as rivers, which distribute nutrients and sediments as they pass. This life-giving cycle is reason enough for some to regard *Her* (the water cycle) as a divinity. She has moods—calm, soothing, inscrutable, benign; stormy, turbulent, withholding; overflowing, destructive. She changes shape in ways that elude us. Leopold: "Rivers are far from simple. In fact the mathematics of hydraulics and sediment movement, for instance, have become so complex that even many experts find them difficult to understand."

Each rill, spring, stream, creek, or river might be a local divinity, difficult to understand. India is famous for river deities—always female. These water ladies draw so close to human form (in sculpture and poetry) it is sometimes hard to know whether the lady is flesh & bone or supernatural. In China, folklore and poetry are rich with rain maidens, water spirits, rainbow goddesses, waterfall shamanesses. Edward Shafer's book, *The Divine Woman: Dragon Ladies and Rain Maidens*, a study of T'ang Dynasty poetry's encounter with these semi-divines, opens with, "This book is about permutations ... It tells how drowned girls became goddesses, and how goddesses became drowned girls."

What about North America? What do we know of the waterways that give or withhold indispensable water for us? What do we know of permutations? One discovery Luna Leopold made catches my imagination because it seems so simple. Water velocity increases as rivers move downhill, towards their mouths. Simply put, they move faster. Prior to his studies conventional opinion stated that rivers slowed—"as when the Mississippi River widens and appears to come to a muddy standstill near New Orleans" (*New York Times*). Appearances were wrong. Water divinities are notorious shape-shifters. They are adept at hiding their forms.

Luna Leopold knew the rivers of the American West. He traveled 300 miles down the Colorado in 1965, through the Grand Canyon (where John Wesley Powell, prophet of American water policy, had gone a hundred years earlier). He charted the geology of the river and its canyon, taking careful notes and detailed measurements. Leopold's work is called science. I'd note how close it is to art. Art—science—lifting the unseen, the half-understood worlds into view. He did his work without compromising the complex, deeply mysterious riparian communities he traveled through. He and his predecessor Powell could be those tiny contemplative men you see in boats in Chinese landscape paintings. Furthermore, Luna wrote only about the physical properties of rivers—not their chemistry, biology, or the teeming life of their riparian zones—"no one volume can treat them adequately. I have neither the expertise nor the space for a proper discussion." This from a scientist who learned ecology from his own father, and who lived to be ninety years old.

North Americans have straightened, dammed, dredged, paved, channeled, & rerouted our rivers. Dumped sludge, pesticides, beer cans, agricultural runoff, nuclear contaminants, industrial waste, and pissed into them. Fought over them, named and renamed them, poached from them, drowned in them. Some Americans have also cleaned them up, removed dams, restocked them with fish, fenced them from livestock, legislated their protection, planted native willows, & restored riverbanks. (The American beaver, *Castor canadensis*, its geologic family-range dating from the Oligocene era, has always managed the waterways better than humans.) We North Americans have also made songs and poems about rivers, produced energetic paintings, spine-tingling photographs, and inherited or evolved a strangely gorgeous vocabulary. Meander, bedload, swale. Floodplain, cross-bed, siltstone. My favorite from Leopold's book: *thalweg*, the deepest part of a river channel, or the lowest thread running the length of a streambed. River maidens must dwell there.

HERE IN COLORADO, WITHIN THE CONTEXT OF URBAN HIGH ART, the engineers
Christo and Jeanne-Claude have devised a plan, decades in the making, to produce
an installation along, or over, the Arkansas River. In a high altitude, fragile stretch of
canyon, along Highway 50 between the two towns of Salida and Cañon City, as the
road winds between burgundy, burnt orange, caramel, sage, and chocolate colored
cliffs, they hope to add "Over the River" to their portfolio. This is to be a suspension
of 6.7 miles of blue fabric, held over the riverbed by 1200 steel cables, anchored to the
ecologically sensitive shorelines by 2400 gigantic concrete blocks. The fabric will cover
the river surface, between eight and twenty-five feet above the water, high enough that
rafters can run the river beneath.

I recently drove that stretch of canyon expecting it to be wild, or at least little
populated. It's surprisingly settled. As a historic sign relates, the Ute Indians were
a presence in the dramatically tight canyon for eight thousand years—"or maybe
forever." Ranchers of European descent had arrived by 1870. And in 1882 a refugee
colony of sixty-three Russian Jews, having fled their home country due to the Tzar's
pogroms, arrived. Hoping to make it as farmers under provisions of the Homestead
Act, they founded the town of Cotopaxi, named for a mountain in Ecuador. The 1880s
saw construction of the Denver & Rio Grande Railroad up the east bank. By 1915 the
"Rainbow Route," a road built by prisoners from the state penitentiary at Cañon City,
and named for the kaleidoscopic colors of the soaring geologic formations, ran all the
way through. There are houses, gift shops, ranches, a few lodges, and one or two diners. A motel under construction advertises "bunks, cafe." The river hosts seasonal raft
tours, is banked by scenic turnouts for automobiles, and shelters quiet fly fishermen
in its shallows. There's lots of vernacular or folk art to see along the route, some quite
humorous. I noticed sculptures made of hay-rolls, and a roadside shrine built in the
arched interior of an upended canoe—a shrine to "fish that got away."

Eagles are present, and on the ledges farther up, bighorn sheep. "Over the River" will need approval by a patchwork of agencies, federal, state, and local. Much of the river and its banks are held by Bureau of Land Management, which has established recreation sites with parking lots & signs—

Please be quiet in
residential areas and
around wildlife.

The Migratory Bird Treaty Act and the Bald Eagle Protection Act will need to be circumvented by the Christos. Eagles may very well fly into the Christos' cables, breaking their wings. Bald eagles have been fishing this stretch of the Arkansas since a geological upheaval diverted the river's course southwards, away from what is now Poncho Pass and the San Luis Valley, forcing the waters through the colorful rock below Salida. Christo and Jeanne-Claude are concerned about F.A.A. restrictions on airplanes and helicopters. Helicopters will be necessary to install their art piece; other aircraft will serve for documentary purposes, and to provide art lovers a bird's eye perspective. Waterfowl feed in the Arkansas's calms.

The likely impact on a local population of bighorn sheep makes eco-activists increasingly irritable towards Christo. Bighorn rarely stray far from their native habitat, maintaining "a high degree of site fidelity" as one wildlife biologist put it. Bighorn are already stressed by road building in the Colorado Rocky Mountains, by shrinking habitat, by ranches, tourist raft excursions, antibiotic-laced apple mash provided by Division of Wildlife biologists, and bridge construction on a far smaller scale than Christo's installation. Bighorn are highly susceptible, when stressed, to lung-worm pneumonia, their principal killer. As you drop out of Salida along the highway to Cañon City, a sign welcomes you into Bighorn Canyon.

At the BLM recreation sites:

> The Arkansas River is known for its fine fishing
> opportunities. Fly fishermen are attracted by
> numerous insect hatches, most notably the caddis fly
> emergence in May. Prime fishing occurs during low
> water periods in March, April, May, August,
> September, and October. The Arkansas has
> primarily brown trout and rainbow trout.

The BLM and the Collegiate Peaks Anglers have posted a notice about New Zealand mud snails, one of many invasive species in Colorado that threaten native ecosystems (someone walked in with contaminated boots, and the small snails took opportunistic hold). The signs ask that before you visit another stream, you wash or soak boots or waders in a solution:

50% Water — 50% Formula 409®
Disinfectant-Degreaser

You can alternatively soak your boots in very hot water, or freeze your boots overnight.

The river will bear scars after Christo's bulldozers and cranes have moved on. "Over the River" is scheduled to stand for two weeks, after two years of construction. Christo hopes to draw a half million "art lovers." That's about thirty-five thousand people a day in the canyon. The Christo and Jeanne-Claude website speaks of the installation coming out of the two artists' hearts. It describes how they "prospected" 14,000 miles of Rocky Mountain roads as they searched out a river over which to hang their industrial mega-art. Funding for the project will come not from grants but from sales of artist drawings and souvenir pieces of fabric. We've witnessed something like this before.

When the two artists slung a 1250 foot wide "Curtain" across a Colorado valley near Rifle several decades ago—haunting, even gorgeous as the artist drawings look when they hang in a Denver gallery—heavy winds tore the actual fabric apart within twenty-four hours. Nine tons of orange nylon polymide blew for miles through the valley.

What might seven miles of shimmering "diaphanous" fabric over the Arkansas do to geomorphic forces like wind, temperature, or sunlight? What will be the effect on waterfowl, fish, wildlife, plant-growth? How will the caddis fly respond? Local officials are concerned by the prospect of heavy traffic in a narrow canyon, and emergency personnel have aired their reservations about visitors who climb steep, crumbling, deceptive terrain, across rock formations populated by rattlesnakes. In 2006, on February 15th a truck of uranium ore overturned on a sharp bend near Swissvale, the hamlet where the roadside shrine to lost fish stands. "The Department of Transportation is pretty concerned about a thing like that happening with all those tourists packed into the canyon," a BLM official confided to *The Denver Post*.

If the river or the wind does something unpredictable—as at Rifle—and miles of the Arkansas get clogged by blue fabric, what will it look like? Geomorphology of a river system is delicate. The mathematics elude even specialists, as Luna Leopold observed. Ecology up in Bighorn country is a delicate, highly vulnerable weave of life forms and climates—a "fabric" ecologists sometimes call it. We don't know the basics of this fabric's response to sunlight, wind, temperature change, or sedimentation. We do know the rivers of North America are in trouble. That is one of the reasons Luna Leopold stated for devoting a ninety-year life of scientific study to North America's waterways. How will miles of industrial fabric, and a string of automobiles, buses, and helicopters, alter the many microclimates along the Arkansas? How do you reconstruct a soil that has developed over geological periods, once you remove two and a half thousand concrete blocks?

Now is a good time to recognize that art can be resoundingly Imperialist. It can be as invasive as commerce, industry, mining, tourism, or military adventure. Many of us believe rivers & their curious deities are better celebrated by non-indus ects. Poems & songs have been traditional celebrations, and I doubt a single culture has lived that did not sing of their rivers. Poems meet the riverbank with minimal intrusion, and usually point out something already there but long overlooked—about the water cycle, shy inhabitants of the riparian landscape, the way rushes and reeds tremble, or about trembling events in the human heart.

I'd like to propose a poetry reading, "Over the River," in place of Christo and Jeanne-Claude's installation. (Poetry readings are notorious for drawing small but respectful crowds.) The Southern Rocky Mountains and their river systems—which irrigate millions of square miles—have had poets and singers of note for longer than any of us can imagine. In Frances Densmore's study, *Northern Ute Music*, published in 1922, appears a song that might open the festival. It was recorded by a Ute Indian named Nikavari, singing into a horn on one of those old recording devices that used wax cylinders. Eighty-five years later Nikavari's song seems prophetic of Christo's "Over the River" project.

> a'nagar.....................red
> vi'nunump................wagon
> ku'avi'tsiya...............dust
> ma'rikats..................white man
> pumi'wanupahai.........looking around

BIBLIOGRAPHY

Densmore, Frances. *Northern Ute Music.* Bureau of American Ethnology, Bulletin 75: Washington D.C., 1922.

Leopold, Luna B. *A View of the River.* Harvard University Press: Cambridge, 2006.

Shafer, Edward. *The Divine Woman: Dragon Ladies and Rain Maidens.* North Point Press: San Francisco, 1980.

Christo's proposal, first conceived in 1992, has been in the works for nearly two decades. Behind the delay: legal battles between the lawyers of the artists, various state and federal government bureaus, and activists opposed to the installation. As of July, 2013, two lawsuits are still pending. Coordinating the effort to stop Christo and Jeanne-Claude's project is the improvised group ROAR (Rags Over the Arkansas). ROAR's website (www.roarcolorado.org) carries much more specific information that that of the Christos', which has dropped dates entirely and currently announces installation "for a future August." Jeanne-Claude's death in November, 2009 seems to have reinforced Christo's resolve to see the project through.

"Kwannon Catches Her First No-hitter," Keith Abbott, sumi-e

ZEN & THE PRECEPTS OF BASEBALL

IN ZEN IT HAS BEEN SAID THAT THE BODHISATTVA'S "PLAY" IS SAVING THE WORLD. The questions this brings forth are good. Is Buddhism serious? Is it playful? Is it for grownups, or for children? Should it be fun or gritty and determined? There's something distinctive and alluring that Buddhist ceremony and baseball share: adults play with all the engrossed seriousness of children at something most of the grownup world considers meaningless.

Buddhist practice will not become an integral part of American life until it has transformed and been transformed by a number of specifically American pastimes. Only when it has seamlessly encountered American culture and taken on a popular inflection will it no longer seem an exotic transplant. When will bluejay look more like a Buddhist emanation than Garuda? Casting an eye back to Japan—which had a parallel encounter with imported Buddhist forms—it's clear that the influence of Zen became deeply established through its interaction with the martial arts, flower arrangement (ikebana), archery, architecture, poetry, and tea ceremony (chado). Not to mention pottery, basketry, and cooking. I want to single out tea for a moment though.

Tea as a formal ceremony arrived from China, probably with Buddhist monks, but initially took hold in Japan as a cultivated activity for the samurai and their warlords. As times changed and the power of a merchant class grew, tea transformed into a prestige event convened by wealthy merchants to display the costly, highly decorative, exotic tea equipment they had acquired. Leonard Koren says, "The sixteenth century tea room was much like the golf course of today for Japanese businessmen. It was where wealthy merchants cultivated new business contracts. It was also where warriors sought and consummated political alliances and celebrated battle victories. (All warriors during this period learned the art of tea.)"

Tea only came into its own under the influence of Sen Rikyu (1522-1591), who broke with the tradition of the wealthy, and even scandalized things a bit. He brought to tea the keystone values that pervade it today and make it the prime example of Zen culture: simplicity, spiritual refinement, and the *wabi-sabi* aesthetic in which objects are valued for being unpretentious, ungainly, imperfect, irregular, and made of rustic materials drawn from the peasant village.

Baseball in this country has followed a curiously similar track, perhaps with a more unwashed cast of characters. It started with the brash, Walt Whitman-like sons of Abner Doubleday—a hard-fought game for urban immigrants and unrestrained roughs. By engaging in an exactingly formal ceremony, ferociously war-like "clans" (mostly immigrant populations) could test themselves against one another. Irish and Italians and Poles fought it out on the diamond. Doing so they became Americans. In Whitman's words: "It's our game—the American game. It will take our people out of doors, fill them with oxygen, give them a larger physical stoicism."

Baseball has through its circuitous windings come to be a game played today by flashy, successful, multi-millionaire capitalists, and Major League baseball appears at moments more about costly paraphernalia and lucrative contracts than the game itself. Its audience along the way has gotten skittish and every threat of a new strike by the wealthy ballplayers against the wealthier corporate owners comes accompanied with a warning that the sport itself, at its professional level, may collapse. The spectators may simply turn away in search of more modest pastimes. Perhaps the moment is ripe for a new Sen Rikyu, and a turn to the Zen economy of simple rough pleasures.

Yet the Zen-like approach of simplicity, along with an austere or folksy formalism, has never deserted baseball. In the 1920s there was the cornfield hero of Joe Jackson's day, and big-jawed Scarecrow kids like Bob Feller stepped out of little towns. The Tin Man or blue-collar ballplayer who brings his lunchbox to the park may be a figure of the past, but he still stands at the yearning heart of the seasoned fan and the radio announcer.

Much like the Negro League paralleled professional baseball for decades, even being termed "the shadow league," so too a down-home world of folklore, with sayings reminiscent of Zen koans, stands in as a kind of shadow to commercialized baseball. This would be baseball's wisdom tradition. Leo Durocher, Branch Rickey, and many others, especially the well-known Yogi Berra, have provided a colorful folk spirit based on paradox, humor, and tiny sayings that punch through the anguish of everyday life. "I want a man strong enough not to fight." "When you come to a fork in the road, take it." Is this baseball or is it Zen?

Baseball also has mysterious "cases" (as they are termed in Zen literature). Did Babe Ruth really point to the seat where his home run would land before swatting it? In the first game of the 1989 World Series did a hobbled Kirk Gibson pulling on his uniform in the ninth inning really tell his coach, *I have one good swing in me*? Did Nansen really cut that cat in half? Was "Cool Papa" Bell so instinctively fast—as his roommate Satchell Paige tells it—he could switch off the light and be in bed before the room got dark?

Is it the wind or the pennant that ripples over Yankee Stadium? Is it your mind?

Here's an important case from the annals of baseball that all practitioners should deeply investigate. They say it happened in 1947 when Branch Rickey, general manager of the Brooklyn Dodgers, brought Jackie Robinson into Major League baseball, breaking the color line. At the Dodger's first game in Cincinnati, on June 21st, a crowd of curious, bleakly hostile, even violent spectators, rose up when the Dodgers took the field, jeering and cursing the first Black player as he stood by first base. Pee Wee Reese, the Dodger's all-star shortstop, walked over to Robinson and dropped his arm over his teammate's shoulder. Just a simple gesture, way ahead of the curve of most of North America. It sobered and quieted the surging crowd.

Hold onto that quiet moment and consider this traditional story. One of the renowned koans of Zen—a case Zen students regularly investigate—comes from the *Platform Sutra* of the Sixth Patriarch, whose name is Hui Neng. Hui Neng, an unlettered janitor, has just secretly received the robe, bowl, and scepter of transmission from his teacher, the Fifth patriarch, Hung-jen. Fleeing the jealous monks of East Mountain monastery, he is pursued by one particularly volatile figure, Hui-ming ("by nature and conduct coarse and violent") who believes Hui Neng carries something of inestimable value. As Hui Neng reaches the summit of Mount Ta-yu, Hui-ming, overtaking him in a snowstorm, raises an arm to strike a murderous blow. Hui Neng cries, "Quick! Not thinking good or evil, what was your original face before your parents were born?" Hui-ming stops dead in his tracks with a satori experience.

Perhaps after "What is the sound of one hand clapping?" this question, "What is your original face?" is the most renowned bit of Zen folklore.

Now return to St. Louis, June, 1947. There stands Pee Wee Reese, having spontaneously stepped over to his teammate Jackie Robinson, a man whose heroism is still untested. Pee Wee slings his arm around the man he shares infield duty with. What does the gesture say to that jeering, deluded crowd? "Quick! Not thinking good or evil (black or white) what was your original face before your parents were born?"

Where does an American go now to find the Zen economy in baseball I spoke of earlier? Is it still with us? I suspect much of its spirit has drifted south of the border—another "shadow" league—to Mexico, El Salvador, Cuba, and the Dominican Republic. Yet it stays here with us too, on the sandlots where children play. Children approach baseball as a practitioner approaches meditation—I mean, it is not preparation for anything, it is not rehearsal. They pursue the endless perfectibility of form. Just as in Zen you sit to be a sitting Buddha, children when they play baseball aren't on their way somewhere. They play ball to be ballplayers.

Remember March and early April, 2001, when the Taliban rulers of Afghanistan first threatened to destroy all Buddhist images in their country, including the enormous cliff carved Buddhas at Bamiyan—and then, in the face of protest from the world, did destroy them? I kept trying to explain to my daughter and her friends what it would mean to have treasures or edifices comparable to those destroyed in North America (this was before September 11th). The closest thing I could think of was what if some administration tore down Yankee Stadium (the house that Ruth built), Fenway Park, or Wrigley Field. In a country as raw, youthful and full of immigrant peoples as the United States, what else has so focused the aspirations of an entire population? I think we've moved past the period when Ellis Island held our gaze. Immigrants no longer come through Ellis Island, and I do not believe the Statute of Liberty reflects what the New York City tourist board wants you to think. More and more I wonder if baseball parks don't provide the most solid emblem of human aspiration.

When the Boston Red Sox picked up Pedro Martinez in the late 1990s, the acquisition brought the enormous Dominican Republic populations in the United States—Americans, but still Dominicans—to the ballparks. Across the country, former Dominicans are fans of the Red Sox. It's a little bit like the 1970s when Roberto Clemente galvanized the African-American population and suddenly there existed a team, the Pittsburgh Pirates, that seemed everything the nation once promised. Baseball, regularly played by immigrants, brings focus to the hopes, the dreams, the pain, the aspiration, the disappointments, of an entire culture. How far is it from those old cliff-carved Buddhas in Bamiyan? What must they have done for caravan riders who braved the Hindukush as they made their way for the Gangetic Plains of India? Already Fenway Park is a destination for pilgrims. Jacoby Ellsbury, Stan Musial, Willy Mays populate the North American imagination alongside figures like Betsy Ross, Ishi, or Mother Jones.

Baseball—ceremonial and formal in its own way as a tea ceremony. Yet year after year unpredictable. Every year when the season heads into October weighty questions crop up. I would ask those who observe professional baseball: Is this the year for the Boston Red Sox? Will the curse of the Bambino ever lift? Can Pete Rose find reprieve and return to baseball? Might a Chicago Cubs player ever display a World Series ring? Underneath lie more pressing questions. Can baseball rediscover its folkloric precepts and take the fork in its own road? Will it relocate its native simplicity and turn out sages again—living buddhas—the likes of Satchel Paige, Pee Wee Reese, Mariano Rivera, or Buck O'Neil?[1]

To the Buddhist I'd turn and ask: Is there any American piece of turf that shares a closer kinship with the meditation hall than the baseball park? How far apart stand the mythologies of Zen and the national pastime? Is there a mind in which the two diamonds—that of Buddhist enlightenment and that of your nearby ball field—overlap? One or two hundred years down the road might we hope for an answer?

In 2003 when I wrote this essay, several of these questions reached towards baseball's vanishing point. Two of them were resolved the following year. The Boston Red Sox fought back in the 2004 playoffs to humiliate the New York Yankees, and went on to win a World Series for the first time since they'd traded Babe Ruth. I leave the questions as they stood though; they are part of baseball's folklore and point towards the hidden precepts.

THE REAL PEOPLE OF WIND AND RAIN

FOR NEARLY FOUR DECADES JOANNE KYGER HAS BEEN WRITING what I think the best poetry our raw, optimistic, troubled North American civilization has to offer. Her poems, her classic 1960s journals of travel in Japan and India, the journals from Mexico that reach up to the present millennium, provide keen examples of how to live "close to the bone." To have a feel for the land—as she does—means to use earth's resources wisely. Which means in poetry to stay close to dry humor, ordinary speech, and finely tuned understatement. Outside the poem, it means to pack lightly, to live on the earth with precision, and then to turn each day of the calendar year into a celebration of "the real people of wind and rain."

I took that last phrase from a poem she recently published, and eyes suddenly wet can't tell if I'm laughing or weeping, that someone has seen the spirit of our American land so clearly.

It seems to have happened in the blink of an eye, but for thirty years I've given myself to two pursuits: poetry, and the values of this North American land. How long ago did a few of us begin asking these questions: Where do you get poems that celebrate this continent? How can a poem fit our spirit as truly the North American forests and mountains we love? When will our poetry show the best of our life, the way poems of T'ang Dynasty China or Edo Japan did? Will someone in the next century look back and say, yes! Those American poets, they really saw something! Yes, that's what it was like to live in those days, and on that land.

I'll put my cards on the table. The only poetry that can be a voice from the American land will be one that enacts an ecology. One that feels as biologically complex as a cubic inch of our underfoot soil. That delves into linguistic equivalents of metabolic pathways, and that tracks the shape-shifting selves that come and go through the poem. Of the many things I've learnt from Joanne Kyger's poetry, maybe the most lovely is that when a poem is open, and begins to look like an ecosystem, unexpected creatures just show up. "The most fun," pioneer conservationist Aldo Leopold wrote, "lies in seeing and studying the unknown."

When it comes to a poetry that yearns to be nature literate, and to sing from the North American land—along with Kyger I think of Gary Snyder, Lorine Niedecker, Peter Blue Cloud, Leslie Marmon Silko, Jack Collom, and now there have emerged dozens of others—these people instinctively know that language is not something we use like a clever tool. Language is far more complex, more like an ecosystem. So, it turns out, is the self. Self and language: almost inseparable, both comprised of metabolic pathways, food chains, principles of germination, of growth and decay, and fields of biological activity. The prairies, Aldo Leopold told us in *Sand County Almanac*, were once a succession: soil-oak-deer-Indian. They became under Euro-American farming practices and industrial agriculture another progression: soil-corn-cow-farmer. If you read into her poems and journals closely, you'll see how attuned Joanne Kyger is to these sorts of who-is-eating-who relationships. It is extraordinary drama—*high noon on the food chain*—when you begin to notice such things.

Joanne's poetry opens to a kind of wry companionship with animals and plants; it watches them eat and get eaten; then it scavenges or feeds on dream, song, old time stories, the weather. Poetry as open, as folkloric as this, typically gets ignored or on occasion trashed in the urbane world of *The New Yorker* and *The New York Review of Books*. But even those Manhattan literary people, editors and publishers, pitch their homes on their own living rock, and we each have our kitchen middens, compost piles, shell mounds, cemeteries, and junk heaps that contain our life secrets and sprout new growth.

Charles Olson's 1959 essay "Projective Verse" is an irrevocable touchstone for American land-based poetry of the last fifty years, and a defining manifesto for much of the interesting poetry that has appeared over that span. In this short space I couldn't begin to summarize its many discoveries—key among them that the poem is a function of the human body, it takes shape from the breath, recording what the eye sees, and letting the mind move actively forward at the moment of writing. But I'll urge you to go back and reread it. Read it first as a document of ecology. Read it second as one of the few useful roadmaps for how contemporary poetry gets written: *one perception must directly and immediately lead to a further perception.* Place that alongside Aldo Leopold's dictum, *Only those able to see the pageant of evolution can be expected to value its theater, the wilderness.* Then having tuned your eye and ear, turn to Joanne Kyger.

In a poem of Joanne Kyger's, all elements on the page hold equal significance. There's no 'message' you can lift out, separate from the palpable, physical occurrence of each word, each imprint of type on the page. Fields of energy make the poem sing. You can't paraphrase it anymore than you can paraphrase the wind or a rainstorm. It is this parallel with the principles of ecology—with the actual events of nature—that strike me as so authentic & contemporary. Kyger is not alone in such poetry-fieldwork, nor in what poets of her generation call 'composition by field'. But the wry humor, the naturalist's eye, the attention given local critters, their feeding or mating habits, their migratory impulses, & the commitment to her bioregion's botany—these set her apart.

Curious how the bounds or margins of the self—and then of the poem—loosen up when you spend a few decades reading aboriginal lore or Buddhist texts, as Joanne Kyger has. And clambering around some of the planet's ecosystems, field guide in hand. As the self gets loose this way, and a shaggy fabric of perception, dream, news, weather report, & friendship, come to give it shape—figures of the local biota just seem to slip through. Wasn't it Jaime de Angulo who noticed that wild creatures are awfully shy, but do get curious about us humans, and like to come around for a look when we do something wild ourselves?

Kyger herself is deeply dug into her own local biota, its phenology and its history: a former fishing-economy village along the coast north of San Francisco, from which she writes and has sagely noted world affairs for four decades.

Think ahead, 100 years from today to November 11, 2092. Is
California still California? Is there a "United States?" And probably this house will be quite close to an ocean view at the rate the
cliff is eroding. There will still be a limited amount of water, but the
septic tank problems will finally be solved.

Such digging in, "reinhabitation" in Peter Berg's well-coined term, is likely to
draw readers from the future, curious to know how we lived and what it is that we
specifically passed on to them. Since the Voices from the American Land series takes
much of its inspiration from the writings of Aldo Leopold, I want to leave off with a
few of his dicta—thoughts against which to read Joanne Kyger's poetry.

> . . . the most fun lies in seeing and studying the unknown.
>
> To those devoid of imagination, a blank place on a map is a useless waste;
> to others, the most valuable part.
>
> Only those able to see the pageant of evolution can be expected to value
> its theater, the wilderness, or its outstanding achievement, the grizzly.

Leopold did make another comment, of such dead accuracy it's eaten at me for
years. Poets, he said, "go pawing over old mythologies,"—notice the taxidermist feel
of *pawing*—"and neglect the great *epics* of *evolution* and the grand *theater* of *ecology*."
Chew on those terms awhile (my italics: epic, theater, evolution, ecology). Think how
they open a passage for us complicated hominids into deep time, and you may glimpse
the ambitious rightness of the Voices from the American Land project.

Aldo Leopold died in 1948. Joanne Kyger that year was a restless, yet-to-be-fully-
trained writer in a Santa Barbara high school. I think Leopold would be profoundly
happy, relieved, maybe exhilarated, to know that poets of her generation have trained
their attention to exactly those studies in ecology and evolution he thought poets of

his day missed in favor of Mediterranean, Arthurian, Norse, or Confucian mythologies. I'll close with his best-known adage, as it catches something I find persistently in Joanne Kyger's poetry. It may give a hint of why we read poetry at all.

> *A thing is right when it tends to preserve the integrity, stability, and beauty of the biotic community.*

Mural painting, Ajanta Cave

SALVAGE ETHNOPOETICS & THE SONGS
OF THE GĀHĀ-KOSA

I

RECENTLY DOING SOME RESEARCH ON BEAR MYTHOLOGY I came on a story recited in 1921 by the Chimariko Indian, Sally Noble, and hand-recorded in a phonetic
script by the ethnographer John Peabody Harrington. That story, translated out of
Harrington's huge store of notebooks by Katherine Turner, is these days called "The
Bear Girl." Distinct to itself, and with its own intimate structure & manner of speech,
it has a theme common to stories about grizzly bear told across the circumpolar north.
Sally Noble's version would have circulated around the drainage system of the Trinity
River of Northern California. Big Bar & Burnt Ranch—along Route 299 which links
I-25 with the coast at Arcata—lie in Chimariko territory, an area mountainous, rich
with wildlife, and still heavily forested. Harrington planned to visit Sally Noble again
the following year, to take down more of her stories & compile further notes on the
nearly extinct local language, but in February of 1922 she passed away, the last fluent
speaker of Chimariko.

What struck me, reading the account of Sally Noble, is a coincidence of dates.
February 1922, the month she died & the Chimariko language lost its final native
speaker, was the month T.S. Eliot's "The Waste Land" appeared. That same year saw
the publication of Joyce's *Ulysses*, the final or complete edition of Rilke's *Duino Elegies*,
and Cesar Vallejo's *Trilce*, which made 1922 a watershed year for Euro-American
Modernism. In obvious ways modern poetry & fiction would never comfortably fit in
old boundaries again. But unknown to most of the urban literary avant-garde, that
era also saw the long-recited stories & poems of numerous cultures quietly disappear.

Franz Boas, from his seat at Columbia University, was desperately training a generation of linguists and anthropological fieldworkers who could go into remote areas (read: undeveloped) with wax cylinder recorders & notebooks, and conserve millennia of lore held in languages threatened with extinction. 'Salvage ethnography' is the term used for the Boasian project—and Boas put his formidable attention, influence, & funding in that direction until the early thirties when the emergence of Nazi power in Europe turned him towards a more visible and immediate threat.

II

I HAVE NO IDEA UNDER WHAT CONDITION THE POEMS OF THE *Gāhā-Kosa* ('Book of Songs') were collected along the drainage of the Godāvarī River in what is today India's Maharashtra State. Whether they got picked up almost accidentally or were part of a deliberate salvage expedition who can say? There exist no records about either the clans or the individuals who composed the songs, under what conditions they sang them, nor for how long or how widely they had been in circulation before ending up in a written manuscript. Even the era that gave birth to the collection is uncertain, with plausible dates ranging from the second century BCE to the seventh century, when the first reference to the collection occurs, ca. 640, in the *Harṣacarita* of the poet Bana. It is certain though, that no fluent speakers of the poetry's original *prakrit,* or dialect, survive into anywhere near our own time.

The traditional view of the songs or poems is that a dynastic chieftain named Hala, himself a good poet and an enthusiast, collected them. His anthology contains seven hundred songs; the anthology's alternate title is *Sattasai,* "Seven Hundred," or in Sanskrit the *Saptaśati.* Forty of the poems are signed "by Hala"—though his own forty stanzas include introductory verses, as well as a summary poem for each of the collection's seven 'books': "here concludes the first" (or second, &c.) "gathering of 100 poems." Less than half the poems are credited by name; yet ascribed poets include more than 250 individuals, some of them women, and their names suggest a range of working people. They are blacksmiths, potters, farmers, not members of the professional literary class known to the classical India of Kalidasa. In India the collection is regarded as older than the poetry of classical Sanskrit—typically it is considered 2000 years old—which places it in the Satavahana Dynasty.

The Satavahana Dynasty lay south of the Vindhya range, a mountain barrier which forms a geographical and political boundary between North India's heartland of Sanskrit culture and the south which resisted colonization for centuries. The Satavahana are the people who created the exquisitely delicate Buddhist cave-frescos at Ajanta, possibly the best-known Indian art outside the South Asian subcontinent. It is tempting to imagine these poems held a central role in whatever ceremonies took place inside the caves, but the poems are notable for their secularism, and the complete lack of supernatural, religious, or mystical motifs. No ghosts, no bodhisattvas, no dreams, no visions, one or two local deities, no mention of the quest for enlightenment, and a solitary novice monk, that's all.

Of Hala nothing is known but his book. The poems he collected are for the most part erotic: playful & discrete, never lascivious, surely a gathering of love poetry equal to any culture's. Later Sanskrit critics, who regarded the *Gāhā-kosa* as a book of origins—standing at the inception of their tradition—decided that each and every poem must contain at least a veiled erotic meaning, and they went to great lengths to analyze every poem—whether about animals, forests, tradesmen, or poverty—to find some possible inflection that pointed towards erotic love. A few critics read every poem for a veiled spiritual intent. At the outset of the collection (as it comes to us today from the various manuscripts), Hala had written in verse—

> You'd think
> from their speculations
> they were adepts
> at love

73

Have they no shame
not to read not even listen
to deathless
prakrit poetry

Editions of the poems have come for centuries with accompanying translations into classical Sanskrit. Since no grammars or lexicons exist for the earlier *prakrit* (often thought to be a 'literary' dialect, whatever that might mean in a context that was likely oral at first) people who read the poems now do it with one eye on the Sanskrit. Each poem has about thirty-two syllables—measured in quantitative mātrikās such that the precise number of syllables can vary a little. This meter was called Āryā, 'noble lady,' when it showed up in Sanskrit, and is pretty close to the standard śloka of epic poetry.

I've been intrigued a long time by two things. First is the large number of anonymous poems. Second, the regularity of meter. Two recent scholars have offered a revised date for the collection, quite a bit later than the traditional 2000 year old time frame, placing it in the seventh century, and they consider it a far more self-conscious collection than what it looks like: a gathering of poems collected in small rural villages or even among tribal people. The settings are certainly rustic: small farming communities laid out along tributaries of the Godāvarī, and hunting tribes—people of the bow—living back in the rugged scrubby highlands where the first tributaries of the Godāvarī River originate.

As to the large number of anonymous poems, their presence squares poorly with the notion that the collection is a later, self-conscious romance-collection written to conjure 'primitive' peoples. Some scholars think the anonymous poems could have been written by women, courtesans of Hala's court. Others that the songs truly were, as Hala himself says, collected from millions of poems or songs extant in his day— that he was a connoisseur of folksongs and oral poems recited around his kingdom.

Was he an early 'salvage ethnographer,' like Boas, Harrington, Alfred Kroeber, Dorothy Demetracopoulou, and others of that period? Certainly if this was the case, Hala could have been a translator as well, or he could have supervised a workshop of scholar-translators at his court. Like Boas he could have sent colleagues into the field, to visit particular tribes or regions, and to collect texts.

The uniform meter throughout the *Gāhā-kosa* suggests there existed a single customary stanza to which the old songs were put—though we may never know if the stanza existed in one or several dialects, or whether they might have been sung to a single or to numerous tunes. On the written page—whether *prakrit*, English or another language—the poems hold an Imagist lucidity. Very likely in performance though, the singers would have stretched out the lyrics at length, and wrapped the "meaningful" words with meaningless vocables, non-sensical sounds, the way actors recited poems in classical Sanskrit theater, or on the model of Native American song, or Japanese *waka*. (Waka as a form occurs in thirty-one syllables, a prime number, a whisker shorter that the *Gāhā-kosa's* thirty-two: India cultivates symmetry, Japan the asymmetric.) The traditional Sanskrit accounts of these poems, which go back more than a millennium, do not say whether Hala or his court poets—or a whole literary scene we know nothing of—made a point of recording local songs which they found in foreign dialects. Possibly they not only translated from tribal languages or non-literary dialects, but set their new poems to a single stanzaic form popular at Hala's court.

Walter Benjamin wrote that literary works do not come into their fulfillment until they have been translated. He called this emergence from their regional or local existence the "afterlife" of a poem, a term which sits intriguingly alongside Hala's phrase about *amrita* (deathless) dialect poetry. In our current century—with so much renewed ethnic and religious conflict, and with real caution about the imperialist agenda behind so many translations—there's wariness about taking other people's poems and simply dropping them into a dominant Euro-American (now global) mainstream tradition. Yet, much song, poem, or story has no life except in translation, since the languages no longer have listeners.

My entry to the poems of Hala's anthology came through Sanskrit. They'd already been translated into a cosmopolitan, colonialist, mainstream tradition from their regional tongue well before English, French, or Russian took over as the receiving languages. At least two translations into English were made by Indian scholars during the twentieth century, in wordy explanatory prose—an effort to salvage precise meaning, catching little of the fleet lexical brilliance, metric dance, or power-of-song of the original. When I started work on poems of the *Gāhā-kosa* in the early nineteen-eighties I had seen no verse translations (there are several now, one of them translating all seven hundred of Hala's book). The strange thing is—the paradox—that those poets or singers we know so little about, have caught some precise emotions—joys, torments, conflicts, tiny gestures of affection—that edge close to modern sensibilities. Poems, then, not just of a western outback territory of the South Asian subcontinent, but instantly recognized cries of the species. For those of us in North America, they present a swift paced expression—full of notable humor, suffering, sexual buzz, & elegance—that at times has been absent from our own poetry, except in underground, marginal, or 'pop' traditions.

•

Kika Silva, a poet at Naropa University's Jack Kerouac School from 2000-2002, asked if she might translate two dozen of my North American versions into Spanish, thinking they would come as welcome news to her Venezuela homeland. With no active speakers left of the *Gāhā-kosa's* original tongue, it seemed clear the poems deserved that sort of afterlife. The following eight pages give Hala's *prakrit*, my American translation, and Kika's Spanish version.

BIBLIOGRAPHY

The Prākrit Gāthā-Saptaśatā, Compiled by Satavahana King Hāla. Edited by
Radhagovinda Basak. The Asiatic Society: Calcutta, 1971.

Andrew Schelling. *Dropping the Bow: Poems from Ancient India.* Revised edition. White
Pine Press: Buffalo, New York, 2008.

—————————. *The Cane Groves of Narmada River: Erotic Poems from Old India.*
City Lights: San Francisco, 1998.

7:18

एक्कल्ल-मओ दिट्ठीअ मइअ तह पुलइओ सअण्हाए ।
पिअ-जाअस्स जह धणुं पडिअं वाहस्स हत्थाओ ॥

Lone buck
in the clearing
nearby doe
eyes him with such
longing
that there
in the trees the hunter
seeing his own girl
lets the bow drop

Anonymous

Venado solitario
en el claro
la hembra, próxima
lo mira con tanto
deseo
que allí
entre los árboles el cazador
viendo la imagen de su amada
deja caer su arco

Anónimo

4:51

जाओ सो वि विलक्खो मए वि हसिऊण गाढमुवगूढो ।
पढमोसरिअस्स विअंसणस्स गण्ठि विमग्गनतो ॥

Fingers
under my skirt
and fumbles—me laughing
squeezing him closer—
strains at
the knot already
untied

Chandra

Dedos
debajo de mi falda
y tropiezan—
yo riéndome
apretándolo más cerca de mí—
forza
el nudo
ya
destado

Chandra

3:31

तस्स अ सोहग्ग-गुण अमहिला-सरिसं च साहसं मज्झ ।
जाणइ गोला-ऊरो वासा-रत्तोदध-रत्तो अ ॥

Only
the swollen waters
of Godāvarī River
and the nights and midnights of rain
have seen
his good luck
and my
unladylike
daring

Makaradhvaja

Solamente
las agues
crecidas del Río Godāvarī
y las noches y
medias noches de lluvia
han visto
su Buena suerte
y mi desafío
impropio de una dama

Makaradhvaja

4:35

बहल-तमा हअ-राई अज्ज पउत्थो पई घरं सुण्णं ।
तह जग्गेसु सअज्जिअ ण जहा अम्हे मुसिज्जामो ॥

Pitch black
the night and I
dread it,
husband's off traveling—
Neighbor
stand watch with me
I fear what happens
in an empty
house

Abhaya

84

Oscuridad profunda
la noche y yo
le temenos
el marido está viajando—
Vecino
permanence en vigía commigo
temo lo que pueda pasar
en una casa vacía

Abhaya

5:8

जार-मसाण-समुब्भव-भूइ-सुह्-प्फंस-सिज्जिरङ्गीए ।
ण समप्पइ णव-कावालिआइ उद्धूलणारम्भो ॥

Dusting her
body with
ash from the burning ground,
to join
the Order of Skulls—
but legs, arms,
too touched with pleasure,
sweating the ash off,
these are her own
lover's cinders

Hala

Cubriendo
su cuerpo con cenizas
de la tierra calcinada,
para unirse así ha
el Orden de Calaveras—
pero piernas, brazos,
también los untaba con placer,
lavando con su sudor la ceniza,
éstas son las cenizas
de su amante

Hala

1.98

रमिऊण पअं पि गओ जाहे उवऊहिउं पडिणिउत्तो ।
अहअं पउत्थ-पइआ व्व तक्खणं सो पवासि व्व ॥

He gets up from
the mat
after we make love
and steps into the moonlight
just for a moment
it's as though he's vanished into
some unimaginably
far off country

Makaranda

Él se levanta
de la estera
después de que hacemos el amor
y camina en la luz de la luna
Solo pore se instante,
es como si se hubiese desvanecido
en un inimaginable y
lejanos país

Makaranda

7.93

दटूण हरिअ-दीहं गोसे णइ-जूरए हलिओ ।
असई-रहस्स-मगगं तुसार-धवले तिल-च्छेत्ते ॥

Out in the fields
at dawn
he leans on his plow
studies the fresh green tracks
in the snow-white sesame flowers
and thinks of her
leaving
his bed before sun up

anonymous

Al amanecer, afuera en el campo
el se apoya en su arado
estudia las huellas frescas y verdes
en las flores de ajonjolí, blancas como la nieve
y piensa en ella
marchándose
de su lecho antes de que amaneciera

Anónimo

5.35

कत्थ गअं रइ-बिम्बं कत्थ पणट्टाओ चन्द-ताराओ ।
गअणे वलाअ-पन्ति कालो होरं व कड्ढेइ ।।

Where has the sun gone?
have moon and stars
vanished?
Black clouds
mount along the horizon
and like an astrologer's mark
a line of white
cranes

anonymous

¿A donde se ha ido el sol?
¿Han desaparecido la luna y las estrellas?
Nubes negras
remontan el horizonte
y como el trazo de un astrólogo
una línea de garzas blancas

Anónimo

OIL & WOLVES

WHEN I HEARD OF JONATHAN SKINNER'S PUSH to get poets engaged with their Congressional representatives, it felt that a possibility—in the air for some time—had come to fruition. For years I have sent letters to government officials on land-use in the West. I've written Senators, members of the House, Forest Service officials, BLM staffers, state governors, local newspapers, and the White House. One letter to a BLM district official—regarding a proposal by artists Christo & Jeanne-Claude to "wrap" a five or ten mile stretch of the Arkansas River—is included in my book, *Wild Form, Savage Grammar.* (I also had a poem addressing the same proposal printed as a broadside by Brad O'Sullivan, and a few of us posted these as an act of political intervention in Salida, Colorado, and along the contested stretch of the Arkansas.)

On nearly every occasion, after sending a communication to an elected or appointed official, I received the expectable form letter in response. Generally the replies thank you for comments, maintain that public officials rely on feedback from their constituency, observe that the issues are complex, and promise that staff is looking into the matter. The Forest Service and BLM have been good, I want to acknowledge, about follow up. This includes sending environmental impact documents, land-use proposals, and sometimes multi-year impact studies along with maps.

When newly elected President Barack Obama appointed Ken Salazar (of my home state, Colorado) Secretary of the Interior—and when Salazar disappointed many of us by holding to the Bush administration's intent to de-list wolves from the endangered species list in the Rocky Mountain West—I sent my first poem to an elected official.

TO THE SECRETARY OF THE INTERIOR

Dear Secretary Salazar,
Here in your home
state Colorado
polls show the population
largely in favor of reintroducing
the Gray or Timber Wolf to our
mountains. I once wrote
that I hoped my children would live
to hear the wolf howl some day.
Word has it you are working to
remove the wolf from Federal protection
and hope shortly to delist it
from the Endangered Species Act.
This leaves as you know wolf
management in the hands
of ranching interests, and as a federal court
noted, does bypass proper scientific
study of whether the Northern
Rocky populations are viable.
I want to suggest
that should you remove
protection, and many of Idaho's wolves
disappear under the guns of mid-level bureaucrats,
we request the Teton Lakota rename
their winter month 'Moon when the
wolves used to run,'

and petition the *Farmer's Almanac*
to delist January as Full Wolf Moon—
they could rename it Moon of
Political Payback,
Aerial Gunning Moon
or Full Moon of the Rancher's Lobby.

Wolves and petrochemicals are intimately connected. The first link: simply that
as natural gas exploration and the construction of wells surge throughout the country,
predator habitat and intact ecosystems are threatened. When wells get drilled, roads
and heavy equipment enter less developed habitat; small but detectable explosions
occur under the earth's surface; and large shy predators are notable as among the first
native species to register stress, dislocation, or disease.

Another maybe less visible connection of oil & wolf, is that beyond any single
issue—shale oil, methane gas drilling, wolf reintroduction, bison management, meth-
amphetamine labs, mountain bike trails, you name it—our concern needs to remain
with policies responsive to the delicate interdependence of air, soil, water, flora, fauna,
and human dignity. Single issues do not exist. Environmental concerns "should echo
and reecho against each other," as Jack Spicer observed about poems.

Likely that wolves
have already
returned to Colorado the news source says
shall we consult oracles
scat on the High Lonesome Ranch—
we're learning to read prints in the dust
yarrow stalks, coins—

> to change ideas about what land is for
> is to change ideas
> about what anything's for—
> consult dreams, visions now
> radio, bumper stickers

The oracles listed in this stanza are not tongue in cheek. Elected officials may take a moment to reflect on a radio report; they are unlikely to take much stock in a bumper sticker; most will surely miss the ecology of dreams and visions. Yet such old-time methods of seeking counsel have often helped establish public policy among indigenous peoples, back as far as records go. Old-time polity, with counsel that includes other-than-humans, did less damage to North American ecologies than our modern system of reliance on special-interest lobbyists.

My poem *A Possible Bag* (source of the above stanza; second book of an Arapaho watershed series), has included responses to the Deepwater Horizon oil disaster, as well as the high-profile problem of hydrofracking for methane gas. (This is hydraulic fracturing of geological structures below ground, by pressurized pumping of water, sand, and chemical brews.) At present the *New York Times* is running a series of articles on "hydrofracking." Now I'm not much interested—either as a poet who believes poems should include multiple layers of experience, or as an ecology student who tries to keep my eyes on many interwoven species—in merely political or single-issue poems. The background, the untidy mess of human needs & consumption, the response of the animal realm (animal spirit realm?) to our actions; the histories, the economics; the far-off wars visible or clandestine—these all factor in. We need to shake them all up in our bag of possible responses.

Here are a series of stanzas from *A Possible Bag*. The first stands as an elegy to a fine North American poet (with a trained ecological conscience) who died as the Deepwater disaster was dominating newspaper headlines. The second two echo several sources:

Thoreau, an Arapaho Ghost Dance song collected about 1890, a friend's account of
pollution in India, newspaper reports of Deepwater.

> British Petroleum's third
> attempt to stem
> the Deepwater Horizon oil pipe disaster
> has failed so wait until August
> here in the present month
> Leslie Scalapino your
> generosity to post off a careful
> letter dated 20 May and on
> the 28th gone, having transmuted
> shyness into peerless generosity
> a curious awkwardness tailed you—
> inimitable own mode gift

> •

> The crises of ecology
> the loss of archaic language
> & traditions
> not cumbered nor mortified by memory
> aquatic birds sea turtles
> *nuhú' biito'owúú'*
> where is our attorney of the
> indigenous plants the local fauna
> bioregion's mode hews close to story
> yes we tell stories to give
> other-than-humans someplace to dwell

We should wear bird masks
over our shame
dark oily tar over their
bills wings & talons
there's no air in the air here
writes Barsamian from Delhi
just dust, dust & CO
BP tries yet again to cap the torrent,
little word on the great twisting oil plumes
a hundred miles long—
while we sit midway in Incognito Gap
to brood on nuclear energy

In the weeks following Deepwater Horizon, it appeared that if oil-rig companies would take a big hit from the spill, the immediate benefactors would be proponents of nuclear energy. Nuclear—like wind power or the solar collection panels that have begun to cover thousands of acres in the West—carries huge consequences for the land. What seems to have dropped out of consideration is the Thoreau-&-Gandhi-inspired notion of restraint. Few speak of limiting our consumption patterns, or even of balancing it. Instead, a few generations of technocrats seem hell-bent on an ever-elusive "clean energy." I suspect this is one instance of what Lewis Mumford called "technological disguises for infantile fantasies." Here it's the fantasy of getting all the energy we need (loyal petrochemical mother love) without disruption, sacrifice, danger, or delay.

The Siouxland cottonwood died
drought decade & age
such things are animate

inanimate the verbs keep getting more
complex pronouns won't sit still
can't is night
solar farm evil as strip mining
for miles the glass
& silicon collectors cover the San Luis Valley
nothing survives
beneath their shadow, save a few
knotted sagebrush
oh the urban environmentalists clamor
for cheap clean safe energy
as though you could get
something for nothing

Show me an energy source that claims to be cheap, clean, and safe, and I bet there's a cover-up, a gang of lobby interests, or a government bail-out. It was seeing SunEdison's acres of solar panels in Colorado's San Luis Valley—the largest photo-voltaic plant in the United States—that made clear the ecological impact of solar may equal that of strip mining. Recognizing this, a few concerned citizens have banded together in the Mojave Desert to resist the installation of huge solar collectors on their fragile home territory. One casualty of the rush towards solar and wind energy pro-duction is the endangered desert tortoise, which stubbornly resists "translocation"— being moved from home terrain to another habitat to make way for dozens of new energy plants.

Yet, check your pocket notebook or things-to-do list. My own begins and ends with fossil fuel dependence.

Change oil in Subaru
repair leak in roof
look up "polysynthetic languages"
practice Arapaho verbs
email Shin Yu
find Kroeber's book hardcover
there are things to do
inside the poem outside
the mask: get bar-oil for
chainsaw

A singular word from the Arapaho language begins to assert itself. Translated as "crazy," it would fit fine with Ezra Pound's term "contra naturam."

That which is *hohóókee*
contrary to the growth of new grass
it's like being a ghost or cadaver
or driving the Interstate through Wyoming
"those people
sometimes they get tricky"
said Chief Sharp Nose of the
government agents
BP collecting surface oil with massive booms
their officials "are going to look very closely for
fraudulent claims"
rescue workers shut from the burn sites
reports of sea
turtles burning alive—

The final lines make me nervous. How topical should a poem be? Luckily Jonathan Skinner writes me that what was "so refreshing and powerful about Allen [Ginsberg] was that he totally said fuck you to the cultural propriety, modesty, and shame, that keeps us all separate in our respective warrens cultivating our atomized scenes." I remain skeptical about reading poems to our Congressional representatives though. I'd prefer a "walk through."

A coalition of local groups—one of which I've been active with—are contesting a ski resort's right to expand into Forest Service wetlands that seem crucial moose habitat. My experience of the district USFS ranger, who may prove a key player here, is that she would be pretty impervious to poems. Her thirty years in the service probably haven't provided much incentive for literary study. But a walk through the critical terrain with a few ecologists, citizens, and poets might prove eye opening. If we get her out on that north-facing slope, I promise Jonathan I'll read her a poem. But here I'll note that ski lifts, water pumps for snow-making, the siphoning of a watershed's run-off from the nearby creek, big Cats grooming the runs at night, and the arrival of increased numbers of skiers by car and airplane, all have instrumentally to do with assumptions about the North American right to use oil.

The dark secret remains: one's dependence on fossil fuels persists, even in rural districts, even burning wood for heat or cooking, even clearing out lodgepole pines killed by the mountain bark beetle.

> With hydraulic wedge & a Honda gasoline motor
> to split the Siouxland cottonwood
> *héétnoo3ítooné3en*
> dense repetition of solar energy
> how it bursts from the grain
> I'm going to tell you a story—
> you cannot go straight into tree's heart
> not even with twenty tons force
> heartwood is gnarled

knotted darkly tangled uncertain
it's how all things grow
the heart has snarled deformations
dark thoughts
here, under the grain of things

Hydro-fracking is now part of everybody's neighborhood, not just in the mountain West. The fortunes of threatened species appear to twist and turn, often in response to energy use and federal policy. This is the era naturalist Peter Warshall called The Great Dying; era of habitat loss, climate disruption, species extinction. The fortunes of the energy companies shift with unnerving speed. In recent years have come Deepwater Horizon; Fukushima Daiichi; Lac-Meganic, Quebec; Keystone XL; al-Qaeda in Yemen. What do the clapping oracles tell us? Those who have worked for the return of the timber wolf, for our home turf's ecology and for the wolf's inherent beauty, often feel we're drawing to an inside straight.

"I saw them crossing
the dirt road in front of my car
one missing a hind foot
walking on bone
the narrow canyon between Woody Creek
& Lenado
I have two theories
one they are secretly
being reintroduced
two that they were
never fully eradicated
I have evidence to support this
it is not public information"

A View from North America:
Mirabai, Lal Ded, and Jayadeva

Mirabai

My work with the poetry of India has largely been through Sanskrit, a wide-ranging, elegant, complicated language, connected long ago to Greek, Etruscan, and Old Irish. The Sanskrit word-hoard is a vast, archaic vocabulary, which anyone can access through a dictionary; it yields images from our nomadic past, compounded words of great subtlety, etymologies that transport you to far dimensions, and a seriously learned approach to wild nature and human nature. A trip to India in 1973 when I was a young man set me to the endless task of translation, and I've lived with Sanskrit's shapely old poems and its intimate vocabulary ever since. For ten or fifteen years I never gave a thought to working with India's medieval song traditions, which occur in languages related to Sanskrit but different enough to require a whole other set of skills.

Then in 1985 the United States government announced a year-long Festival of India. This was kicked off with an official series of events—culturally quite wide-open, considering the temper of Washington, D.C. at the time, which was irrationally fearful of immigrants, communists, hippies, drug users, socialists, poor people, atheists, environmentalists, and artists. The Festival began with a "street market" on the Mall in Washington. Musicians, jugglers, acrobats, camels, ox-carts, turban-wearing craftsmen, sari-clad dancers, even entire museum exhibits were brought from India. Musician Ravi Shankar gave the inaugural concert to an audience that included U.S. President Ronald Reagan and high-ranking senators and lobbyists from inside what we call the Beltway.

Back in Berkeley where I was living at the time, my friend Philip Barry, manager of Shambhala Bookshop on Telegraph Avenue, pulled me inside and asked what I knew of Indian poetry. The noise about India—full of art, images, and ideas unfamiliar to most Americans—had provoked a little flurry of interest in poetry. Nobody knew the name of any Indian poet, however, except that of Kabir, whose reputation in North America was based on two books. The first was the *One Hundred Poems of Kabir* translated many decades earlier by Rabindranath Tagore and Evelyn Underhill. That book carries the lingering scent of Victorian parlors, and is based on a manuscript that had surfaced in Bengal but disappeared shortly afterwards. Quite likely none of its poems were composed by Kabir. The other collection was Robert Bly's *The Kabir Book*. Bly had taken forty-four of Tagore's translations and reworked them into colloquial American stanzas. There was a third small collection, but almost nobody was paying attention to Ezra Pound's stately translations of a handful of Kabir poems, done off the versions of Bengali poet Kali Mohan Ghosh and published in Calcutta in 1913. Beyond those three collections there was nearly nothing else in print.

That August the raga singer Lakshmi Shankar gave a concert at St. John's Church in Berkeley, concluding with *bandish* (compositions) by Kabir, Mirabai, Surdas, and one of Tagore's own Bengali songs. I walked around the jasmine-scented fog-cool evening streets of the East Bay for days, high from her performance, and the following week wrote an essay. What I wanted to come to terms with was this tradition, *bhakti* or devotional song, so little heard in North America, so full of instantly recognizable sanity. Without knowing much about the lyrics, but with my head full of music, I could instinctively see a precise tradition of oppositional poetry, close to American styles like gospel, hobo songs, or the blues.

By oppositional poetry I mean songs or poems showing—advocating, pioneering—a way of life that runs counter to prevailing civic good sense. Most social assumptions are in some fashion complicit in what Karl Marx called "false consciousness" and American poet Kenneth Rexroth bluntly termed "the social lie." American political reality in the mid-eighties had swung sharply right, and under President Reagan some real loonies were taking charge of public policy. We know Ronald Reagan was a small-minded religious fundamentalist, that he consulted Hollywood-style astrologers, and watched B-grade war movies again and again to decide how he should proceed on the international front. He was dreaming up satellite-mounted lasers in space and talking to his cabinet about the "Book of Revelation." One of poetry's enduring tasks, visible then as now, is to present alternatives to absurd ideas about the necessity of war and to point out inequities in wealth, political influence, or privilege.

However else you might characterize *bhakti* poetry—Mirabai's, Kabir's, and Tagore's, for example—at its base it is love poetry. It sings to a deity who might be a lover, who seems to have as much flesh as you or me. Its premises are anti-war, it is indifferent to commerce, and it tends to expose sexism, racism, classism, and crippling religious authority. *Bhakti* poetry—which until modern times, and a democratization of literacy in India, was circulated through song—doesn't make its opposition through argument. It's more likely to circumvent debate and go direct to the human heart with a politics of eroticism and high-quality nonsense; the sort of nonsense that shows how feeble most social assumptions are. A term taken from Sanskrit poetics is useful: *sandhya-bhasha*, "twilight speech." Twilight speech is imagistic, paradoxical, a-logical, to counter the "logic" of the powerful. I also appreciate the term used of Kabir's baffling paradoxes: *ulatbamshi*, "upside down speech."

These kinds of non-rational speech can communicate with immediacy. Lovers, children, and family members use them all the time. So do Zen teachers, poets, saints, and popular songwriters.

These countertraditions—*bhakti* poetry being one of the world's longest lasting, originating certainly by the eighth century and still alive today—often come to us in the form of song. The *bhakti* poets' *padas* (lyrics) or *bandish* (compositions) get sung in *bhajan* style (when meant to sound religious), or as *thumri* (when meant to sound secular), or as folk song in villages. Quite malleable, they also move readily from language to language in India. They are not really poems at all, and seem, from at least the twelfth century, to have been sung to specified *ragas*. Music—we all know—has effects beyond what the accompanying words say. So does poetry, which can employ techniques similar to music. These have to do with sound, figures, and rhythmic patterns.

Irony, playfulness, teasing. "The meaning always exceeds the words," is the phrase I hold in mind. This is not anti-intellectualism, but a refusal of conventional thinking. And a bow to the old South Asian notion that spirits or intelligences live in human speech—whether we acknowledge them or not. With elegance, humor, passion, and other irrepressible human qualities, the songs of the *bhakti* poets turn the tables on piety and hypocrisy. That's why the songs sound vital today. The same pieties, assumptions, and power struggles wrecking our current world are the ones that tossed Mirabai's world into chaos. Only the cast of characters has changed.

When it came time in 1992 to gather a collection of my essays for a book on India's poetry, my editor, American poet Leslie Scalapino, asked if I would add some translations of Mirabai poems to the essay on *bhakti* I'd written back in 1985. She rightly assumed few Americans would know what the lyrics are like. I told her to reread my essay carefully. I was convinced that *bhakti* was really music, its performance outstripping what the words on their own could say. Go to the musicians, I'd urged—

> They are the ones, not the scholars and theologians (though these have performed fine and indispensable work), who risk themselves on each song. They are the ones negotiating the delicate griefs and savage ecstasies you arrive at through Mirabai's music.

Leslie persisted though. I admire her as a poet and publisher, and finally agreed to try some translation. I remember deciding I would stop at seven poems. My thought was to do ten, and stick with the best seven. I found a silk merchant who lived nearby. He had studied some medieval Hindi in school, and I was grounded in Sanskrit. Together we could converge on Mirabai from two directions. For a few weeks, in the winter of 1992, I would drive out to his rural Colorado neighborhood, park my Datsun below the bluff, and climb up through snow and Ponderosa pines to his house, with a rucksack stuffed with dictionaries. Between us, we collected a number of tapes of

India's singers, including the great Mirabai recordings by M.S. Subhalakshmi, Kishori Amonkar's *bhakti* songs, and Lakshmi Shankar.

Once we got to work—I had managed to acquire several editions of Mirabai's *Padavali*—I saw it might be possible to do more than seven poems. At the time there were really no viable books about Mirabai in English, the main one a literal and disheartingly dry set of lyrics by A.J. Alston. With some further searching I found two other translations. They seemed to bear no resemblance whatever to Subhalakshmi's brave singing or Lakshmi Shankar's haunting *"Jogi mata jaa, mata jaa,"* which is almost an exact counterpart to the blues of "Baby, please don't go." What kind of mistranslation would you get if you took Blind Lemon Jefferson—this was the image that came to me—put his words to literal Hindi, justified them down the left margin, and printed them without his muffled smoky-torn voice and angry plaintive guitar strings?

Yet some of our poems began to work out.

> Binding my ankles with silver
> I danced—
> people in town called me crazy.
> She'll ruin the clan
> said my mother-in-law,
> and the prince
> had a cup of venom delivered.
> I laughed as I drank it.
> Can't they see?
> Body and mind aren't something to lose,
> the Dark One's already seized them.
> Mira's lord can lift mountains
> he is her refuge.

When my comrade the silk merchant dropped away from the project, I found someone nearby teaching Hindi and took classes in earnest for a few months. That was an important part of the work, but only a part. The real task lay with my own language. I had to ask, why do the Mira *padas* look so dead on the page? What is the living heart of these things as songs? Take away the singer and what's left?

One of the most important cues came to me in the middle of the night. I woke with Mira's lyrics in my head and remembered an interview Miles Davis, American jazz virtuoso, gave to *Playboy* magazine back in the sixties. The interviewer, a dweller in the over-heated world of Hugh Heffner, just didn't get cool jazz at all. They were sitting in Miles's living room, where an Alexander Calder mobile hung from the ceiling. At one point Miles, exasperated, swept a hand towards the mobile—"If Calder can make sculpture like that, why can't I make songs move around?" That was a most important insight! Suddenly I saw why translating Mirabai's *text* didn't work. She never had a text, a set of lines strung one after another. The words, images, puns, rhythms, were touchstones, to be set into motion, not fixed into place.

You see, such singing works by phrases, winding them around, testing their moods, repeating, varying, suggesting, threading them in delicate colorful ways for the night's performance. To line up Mirabai's *padas*, her "feet," one after another, simply didn't reveal them. Where was the high quality nonsense of song? Now I had permission—from the singers, from Miles Davis—to weave lines into a vivid fabric, as performance. I might need to leave something out, or steal some gesture from a singer, or import the image from one song to another. Going back to the singers, I began to understand the mobility of images, of phrases, and could locate for each composition a central notion that had previously eluded me.

I want to discuss one other insight that came to me around that time. Every language has its own genius, what in India you call a *shakti*—a power, a living sinuous intelligence. "A snake-like beauty in the living changes of syntax," American poet Robert Duncan once wrote. A snake-like beauty! That's the feel you go for. Mirabai knew that the most powerful *shakti* is the one that animates your childhood language. That's the language where the snake-like beauty dwells. In what words do you make love? speak to your children? Your parents? Your neighbors and friends? So I had to find the *shakti* of my own language. If a Mirabai song, in her Rajasthani-Gujerati-Hindi dialect drives a shiver through you, it is only translated when the new poem makes you feel like you've stroked the hood of a cobra. There are beauties in poems that the translator has to leave behind with regret. But every language has its own splendors, powers, gifts of seduction, serpent-like thrills—and you can find "equivalents" to the original if you go deep enough into your own tongue. Again, the meaning exceeds the words.

I managed to turn eighty of Mirabai's lyrics into poems—out of around three hundred that modern scholars have established as authentically hers. That felt like a book. Each of those songs has at least one striking image I could locate at the center, and try to animate with the powers of the spoken (and slightly literary) American vernacular I've picked up in the American West.

My friend Vidya Rao, known for her *thumri* singing, points out that Mirabai has at least three types of "voice," each well defined. There is a defiant voice, a passionate voice, and then come the highly individuated *padas* of her late lyrics, which are smoldering and vulnerable. Vidya says, "There are many shades to Mira's person." She also demonstrates that by moving a lyric from one *raga* to another, or one style of song to another, you change shades of meaning. Are these lyrics ironic, vulnerable, passionate, seductive, defiant? Gesture and facial expressions in the *thumri* form of singing charge the words with complex overtones. Shift those same lyrics into the *bhajan* or devotional style, and what was seductive may become entreating, or even pious.

When it came time to find a final poem—the "gateway" out of my Mirabai book, the taste that would linger in a reader's mouth as he or she took leave—I realized I had to determine which of the voices, which of the moods to select. This felt wide open to me: defiant, passionate, vulnerable, angry, seductive, rapturous. Nobody can establish a firm chronology for Mirabai's songs, so just as the order of lines in a song are malleable, the order of songs in a performance (or a book) is mutable according to a singer's mood. I decided to close my book on a poem of desolation—the raw vulnerability Vidya Rao suggests might be Mira's mature tone. Perhaps finishing with this voice casts a deeper, more believable shadow across the book. Perhaps it leaves the book an open question and protects it from anyone who wants to make Mirabai too holy, too slick. Who knows? Desolation is familiar to all of us.

Drunk, turbulent clouds
roll overhead
but they bring from the Dark One
no message.
Listen!
the cry of a peacock,
a nightingale's faraway ballad,
a cuckoo!
Lightning
flares in the darkness,
a rejected girl shivers,
thunder, sweet wind and rain.
Lifetimes ago
Mira's heart went with the Dark One,
tonight in her solitude
infidelity spits
                    like a snake—

LAL DED

LAL DED WAS BORN IN KASHMIR EARLY IN THE 1300S, probably to parents of
some Hindu persuasion. Her *vākh* (verses, sayings), suggest an early education in her
father's house and eventual marriage into a Brahmin family of Pampor, where her
mother in law treated her with dispiriting cruelty. Lalla, as she calls herself in the signature line of her poems, took to visiting the nearby river each morning—traditional
for an Indian woman who went to fetch the household's water. But Lalla would cross
the river secretly, maybe by ferry, to worship Naṭa Keśava Bhairava, a form of Śiva, in
his temple situated on the far bank. Her mother in law, noticing her long absences,
suspected her of infidelity. Rivers in Indian lore, particularly their shaded riparian
groves and stands of tall, concealing rushes, are in longstanding convention the site of
clandestine trysts.

Lal Ded's husband became soured by his mother's suspicion and one day when
Lalla entered the house with a pot of water on her head, struck it with his staff in a fit
of violent jealousy. The earthenware jug shattered but the water remained "frozen" in
place, atop her head, until Lalla had poured it into the household containers. A little
leftover water she tossed out the door where it formed a miraculous lake, said to exist
in the early 20th century, but dry today.

Lalla's reputation spread, based on a series of miracles she performed. People
began to seek her out for assistance or simply to take darshan, that specifically Indian
practice in which blessings come to a person who ceremonially takes sight of a deity,
a saint, or a spiritual teacher. Lal Ded's love of solitude was compromised by all the
attention and the rancor in her house. She left her graceless marriage and took up the
homeless life. Legend, based on the following verse, has it that she went forth naked,
dancing on the roads, singing her *vākh*.

> My guru gave a single precept:
> turn your gaze from outside to inside

fix it on the hidden self.
I, Lalla, took this to heart
and naked set forth to dance—

One Moslem chronicler says she danced in ecstasy "like the Hebrew *nabis* of old and the more recent Dervishes." Islamic writers chronicle her encounters with their holy men, while Hindu texts tell of gurus. The Kashmir of her day held Buddhists, Nath yogins, Brahmin teachers, Sufis, and Tantric adepts. She may have learnt something from each of them. Still, she seems to have considered herself a dedicated Śaivite yogini (practitioner dedicated to Śiva); tales of insight and supernatural power surpassing that of her instructors began to circulate. Yet records of her don't appear until centuries after her death, nor has anyone found manuscripts containing her *vākh* that date from anywhere near her lifetime.

Circulating oral stories make a good deal of her decision to live without clothing; this made her a spectacle at times. She was taunted. Jane Hirshfield tells a story of children pestering Lalla, and a silk merchant who came to her defense by offering bundles of cloth to cover herself with. Taking two bolts of equal weight, Lal Ded placed one over each shoulder and walked off. "As she went through the day, each time someone ridiculed her, she tied a knot in the cloth on her left shoulder; each time someone praised her, she tied a knot in the cloth on the right. At day's end, she returned to the merchant, and asked him to weigh the bundles. She thanked him for his earlier concern, but also pointed out that, as he could see for himself, nothing had changed." Whether people praised or reviled her, the knotted bundles remained equal in weight.

Around the age of fifty Lal Ded sang some verses and a crowd gathered. On finishing she climbed into a large earthen pot and pulled another over her head. When she did not reemerge the spectators separated the two containers. They were empty.

Beneath you yawns a pit.
How can you dance over it,
how can you gather belongings?
There's nothing you can take with you.
How can you even
savor food or drink?

•

I have seen an educated man starve,
a leaf blown off by bitter wind.
Once I saw a thoughtless fool
beat his cook.
Lalla has been waiting
for the allure of the world
to fall away.

•

Ocean and the mind are alike.
Under the ocean
flames *vadvagni*, the world-destroying fire.
In man's heart twists the
flame of rage.
When that one bursts forth,
its searing words of wrath and abuse

scorch everything.
If you weigh the words
calmly, though, imperturbably,
you'll see they have no substance,
no weight.

●

It provides your body clothes.
It wards off the cold.
It needs only scrub & water to survive.
Who instructed you, O brahmin,
to cut this sheep's throat—
to placate a lifeless stone?

●

I might scatter the southern clouds,
drain the sea, or cure someone
hopelessly ill.
But to change the mind
of a fool
is beyond me.

●

I came by the public road
but won't return on it.
On the embankment I stand, halfway
through the journey.

Day is gone. Night has fallen.
I dig in my pockets but can't find a
cowrie shell.
What can I pay for the ferry?

·

The god is stone.
The temple is stone.
Top to bottom everything's stone.
What are you praying to,
learned man?
Can you harmonize
your five bodily breaths
with the mind?

·

You are the earth, the sky,
the air, the day, the night.
You are the grain
the sandalwood paste
the water, flowers, and all else.
What could I possibly bring
as an offering?

Solitary, I roamed the extent of Space,
leaving calculation behind.
The place of the hidden Self
opened and suddenly
out of the filth
bloomed a lotus.

•

O Blue-Throated God
I have the same six constituents as you,
yet separate from you
I'm miserable.
Here's the difference—
you have mastered the six*
I've been robbed by them.

* The six *kancukas*, "husks" or "coverings" of existence in
Kashmir Saivism: appearance, form, time, knowledge, passion, fate.

•

I, Lalla, entered
the gate of the mind's garden and saw
Śiva united with Śakti.
I was immersed in the lake of undying bliss.
Here, in this lifetime,
I've been unchained from the wheel
of birth and death.
What can the world do to me?

JAYADEVA

THE TWELFTH CENTURY *Gīta-govinda* OF JAYADEVA IS WIDELY REGARDED as the last great poem in the Sanskrit language. It holds two other distinctions. First, it appears to be the first full-blown account in literature of Radha as the youthful Krishna's favorite among the *gopis*, or cow-herding girls, of Vrindavana, the geographic center of Krishna's biography. Second, it seems to be the first historical instance of poetry written with specified *ragas* to which its lyrics are sung. The poem presents the love affair of Krishna and Radha as a cycle, from initial "secret desires" and urgent lovemaking, to separation—nights of betrayal, mistrust, loneliness, feverish longing—and finally to a consummation that is spiritual as well as carnal. At this remove from Jayadeva's century, who can tell if he meant his poetry cycle as an allegory of the human spirit's dark night and final illumination? That is how it gets read though.

Jayadeva's *Gīta* (sacred song) has been called an opera. It is comprised of twelve cantos or chapters, with twenty-four songs distributed through. Narrative verse, composed not in song structure but in classical Sanskrit *kavya* (poetry) form and meter, recounts the storyline. The twenty-four songs, with repeating refrains for each verse, resemble nothing from the earlier Sanskrit tradition. Jayadeva adopted rhythms from folk sources; the songs occur in end-rhymed couplets (almost unknown to Sanskrit court tradition), each couplet then followed by a refrain that sums up the emotion or action of the entire song. You could say Jayadeva's *Gīta* straddles high-art Sanskrit poetry and the local, vernacular traditions. For centuries the *Gīta-govinda* has been performed, especially in Orissa, with dancers, costume, music, and stage settings. It is considered a sacred text, and in the fifteenth century was instituted as the sole liturgy for the enormous Sri Jagannatha temple in Puri on India's east coast.

Jayadeva's birthplace is uncertain—some think Orissa, some Mithila, some Bengal. Accounts of his life say he was a carefully trained poet, in the Sanskrit mode, when he took a vow to wander without home, and sleep no more than a single night under any tree. On this endless pilgrimage he passed through Puri, where the chief administrator of the Jagannatha temple had a vision that Jayadeva should marry his daughter—a dancer dedicated to the temple—settle down, and compose a devotional poem to Krishna. The daughter's name may have been Padmavati—a name that appears in one of the *Gita-govinda's* opening verses. What we know is that Jayadeva complied. He renounced his vows, married the dancer, and wrote his poem.

Meeting Padmavati wakened in Jayadeva the *rasa* of love. His poem never divides the *rasa* into erotic or spiritual modes. What might have seemed distant accounts of spiritual grace, a theme for poetry and folksong, or even an abstract religious doctrine, came alive in his own body: the merging of spiritual and erotic ecstasy. Later poets would sing of the *prem-bhakti-marg*, the path of love and devotion, and warn of its razor sharp edge. But under Padmavati's hands Jayadeva learnt that the old tales, the yogic teachings, were no abstract affair. They are an experience tasted through one's own senses, its rhythms and phases available to anyone.

In Jayadeva's poem, Krishna appears desperately human. An underlying cadence suggests he is the driving force of wild nature—Eros incarnate—but his acutely human emotions give the poem poignance. In another sphere, the cosmic realm of Vaishnava devotion, Krishna remains the final resort for humans in the Kali Yuga, an era when older techniques of yoga, meditation, or worship may be out of human reach. One's own body, wracked as it is by desire and loneliness, is the sole vehicle for salvation and Krishna is one's only refuge. Radha, meanwhile, may be something like a spirit of nature, dancing with anguish and ecstasy in our glands. For her, "erotic" or "spiritual" would be meaningless distinctions as she sets out, spurred by relentless desire, to the dark grove of tamala trees where her lover waits. She is pure life-force, the spirit within us, that yearns to give love in a dark, cruel era.

The following verses, about a tenth of the full poem, mostly draw from the "classical" narrative stanzas. They reveal the cycle of the poem as Jayadeva conceived it.

"Clouds thicken the sky,
the forests are
dark with tamala trees.
He is afraid of night, Radha,
take him home."
They depart at Nanda's directive
passing on the way
thickets of trees.
But reaching Yamuna River, secret desires
overtake Radha and Krishna.

Jayadeva, chief poet on pilgrimage
to Padmavati's feet—
every craft of
Goddess Language
stored in his heart—
has assembled tales from the erotic encounters
of Krishna and Shri
to compose these cantos.

If thoughts of Krishna
make your heart moody;

if arts of courtship
stir something deep;
Then listen to Jayadeva's songs
flooded with tender music.

Krishna stirs every
creature on earth.
Archaic longing awakens.
He initiates Love's
holy rite with languorous blue
lotus limbs.
Cowherd girls like
splendid wild animals draw him into their
bodies for pleasure—
It is spring. Krishna at play
is eros incarnate.

Krishna roamed the forest
taking the cowherdesses one after
another for love.
Radha's hold slackened,
jealousy drove her far off.
But over each refuge
in the vine-draped thickets

swarmed a loud circle of bees.
Miserable
she confided the secret
to her friend—

Radha speaks
　　My conflicted heart
　　treasures even his infidelities.
　　Won't admit anger.
　　Forgives the deceptions.
　　Secret desires rise in my breasts.
　　What can I do? Krishna
　　hungry for lovers
　　slips off without me.
　　This torn heart grows only
　　more ardent.

　　His hand loosens from the
　　bamboo flute.
　　A tangle of pretty
　　eyes draws him down.
　　Moist excitement on his cheeks.
　　Krishna catches me
　　eyeing him in a grove
　　swarmed by young women—
　　I stare at his smiling baffled face
　　and get aroused.

Krishna speaks
　　Every touch brought a new thrill.
　　Her eyes darted wildly.
　　From her mouth the
　　fragrance of lotus,
　　a rush of sweet forbidden words.
　　A droplet of juice
　　on her crimson lower lip.
　　My mind fixes these absent
　　sensations in a samadhi—
　　How is it that parted from her
　　the oldest
　　wound breaks open?

Radha's messenger speaks
　　Her house has become
　　a pulsating jungle.
　　Her circle of girlfriends
　　a tightening snare.
　　Each time she breathes
　　a sheet of flame
　　bursts above the trees.
　　Krishna, you have gone—
　　in your absence she takes shape
　　as a doe crying out—
　　while Love turns to Death
　　& closes in
　　on tiger paws.

Sick with feverish
urges.
Only the poultice of your body
can heal her, holy physician of the heart.
Free her from torment, Krishna—
or are you
cruel as a thunderbolt?

The messenger speaks to Radha
Krishna lingers
in the thicket
where together you mastered the secrets
of lovemaking.
Fixed in meditation,
sleepless
he chants a sequence of mantras.
He has one burning desire—
to draw *amrita*
from your offered breasts.

Sighs, short repeated gasps—
he glances around helpless.
The thicket deserted.
He pushes back in, his breath
comes in a rasp.
He rebuilds the couch of blue floral branches,

steps back and studies it.
Radha, precious Radha!
Your lover turns on a wheel,
image after
feverish image.

She ornaments her limbs
if a single leaf stirs
in the forest.
She thinks it's you, folds back
the bedclothes and stares
in rapture for hours.
Her heart conceives a hundred
amorous games on the well-prepared bed.
But without you this
wisp of a girl
will fade
to nothing tonight.

At nightfall
the crater-pocked moon as though
exposing a crime
slips onto the paths of
girls who seek lovers.
It casts a platinum web
over Vrindavan forest's dark hollows—
a sandalwood spot
on the proud face of sky.

The brindled moon soars above.
Krishna waits underneath.
And Radha
wrenched with grief
is alone.

The lonely moon
pale as Krishna's sad, far-off
lotus-face has
calmed my thoughts.
O but the moon is also Love's planet—
a wild desolation
strikes through my heart.

Let the old doubts go,
anguished Radha.
Your unfathomed breasts and
cavernous loins
are all I desire.
What other girl has the power?
Love is a ghost
that has slipped into my entrails.
When I reach to embrace your
deep breasts
may we fulfill the rite
we were born for—

Krishna for hours
entreated
the doe-eyed girl
then returned to his thicket bed and dressed.
Night fell again.
Radha, unseen, put on radiant gems.
A girlish voice pressed her—
go swiftly.

Her companion reports—
   "She'll look into me—
   tell love tales—
   chafing with pleasure she'll draw me—
   into her body—
   drakshyati vakshyati ramsyate"
   —he's fearful,
   he glances about. He shivers for you,
   bristles, calls wildly, sweats, goes forward,
   reels back.
   The dark thicket closes
   about him.

Eyes dark with kohl
ears bright with creamy tamala petals
a black lotus headdress & breasts
traced with musk-leaf—

In every thicket, friend,
Night's precious cloak wraps a girl's limbs.
The veiled affairs
the racing heart...

Eager, fearful, ecstatic—
darting her eyes across Govinda she
enters the thicket.
Ankles ringing with silver.

Her friends have slipped off.
Her lower lip is moist
wistful, chaste, swollen, trembling, deep.
He sees her raw heart
sees her eyes rest on the couch of
fresh flowering twigs
& speaks.

Sung to Raga Vibhasa

> *Come, Radha, come. Krishna follows your*
> *every desire.*
> "Soil my bed with indigo footprints, Kamini,
> lay waste the grove
> savage it with your petal-soft feet.

"I take your feet in lotus hands, Kamini,
you have come far.
Lay these gold flaring anklets across my bed.
"Let yes yes flow from your mouth like *amrita*.
From your breasts, Kamini,
I draw off the dukula-cloth. We are no longer separate."

Sung to Raga Ramakari

She sings while Krishna plays, her heart drawn
into ecstasy—
"On my breast, your hand Krishna
cool as sandalwood. Draw a leaf wet with deer musk here,
it is Love's sacramental jar.

"Drape my loins with jeweled belts, fabric & gemstones.
My mons venus is brimming with nectar,
a cave mouth for thrusts of Desire."

Reckless, inflamed, she presses forth
to the urgent campaign
of sexual love,
flips over and mounts him,
savors the way
he gives in...

... Later, eyes lidded,
loins cool & no longer rippling,
her arms trail like vines.
Only her chest continues to heave.
Is climbing on top
what brought her victory?

Reader, open your heart
to Jayadeva's well-
crafted poem.
Krishna's deeds lie in your memory now—
amrita to salve
a Dark Age's pestilence.

Coda

On my breast draw a leaf
paint my cheeks
lay a silk scarf across these dark loins.
Wind into my heavy black braid
white petals,
fit gemstones onto my wrists,
anklets over my feet.
And each thing she desired
her saffron-robed lover
fulfilled.

Choson Dynasty, 1392-1910—Collection of Emille Museum, Seoul, Korea

THE *Beat Scene* INTERVIEW
WITH TREVOR CAROLAN
2003

Trevor Carolan: Andrew, topographically you've ranged widely in your career. Born and raised on the east coast; formative years as writer, younger literateur in northern California's San Francisco Bay-Santa Cruz area; and resident for some years now at what's close to the geographic heart of America in the Colorado front range country at Naropa University in Boulder. Any sense of what these three experiences bring to your work?

ANDREW SCHELLING: I could answer this question many ways but let me do it in terms of North American poetry. The East coast, New England specifically, provided a few heroic poetry figures from the past, but the possibilities seemed constricted. Too much Europe, too much English department, too much Ivy League putdown & depression. I wanted something open, lively, archaic, full of wind & granite. I knew it existed on the West coast. Pacific Rim culture, the full impact of Asia, and the encounter with vast stretches of wilderness were what I went west for. I was seventeen years in Northern California where the Sierra Nevada and Coast Range Mountains were my singular teachers, and I could stand on a crest of chaparral looking towards Asia.

Colorado is something different. It represents a move away from the littoral coastlines, away from the influence of across-the-ocean continents, and a move into the nation's heartland. Living here, the Rocky Mountains—spine of our continent—sets the instinctual compass-points north & south. There's a steady Native American influence, then five hundred years of Mexico. Just south of here it was all Mexico until 1848 when the United States did the big land grab called Treaty of Guadalupe Hidalgo and took half of Mexico. In 1994 I looked at a map & realized the poets of Mexico City live closer to me than the poets of New York.

But this Western land. Half of it is public land. It belongs to the United States people and is technically supervised by the Federal government. I'm fascinated by and deeply invested in the conflicts over who gets to use it and how. Is public land for the timber companies, for mining, oil & mineral extractors? Is it for ranchers? Hunters? Hikers & skiers? Indigenous species and threatened plants and animals? Biologists? Is it for the air force to do target practice on, the Feds to test outlandishly destructive weapons? For condominiums? Prairie dogs & coyote? I guess you could say this is where I set up my poetry.

TC: Regarding the East Coast, in your new book Wild Form, Savage Grammar *you allude to Thoreau. How profoundly do you feel he and the New England Transcendentalists have resonated in the American cultural mind? Is Whitman part of this? Any observation on Whitman taking his show on the road—in the sense that, say, Kerouac and Ginsberg would do later as "stenographers of consciousness," as bard-archivists of the nation's life and times?*

AS: Whitman is a great poet. He showed a lot of people the way to break with the formal constraints of European poetry, and to make things out of words that feel like they belong on North American landscapes. I love Whitman. He prophesied the country as we know it today. His America came into existence. This is Walt Whitman's America. Two weeks ago a very conservative Supreme Court surprised everyone by overturning a 1986 Texas sodomy law, effectively saying that whatever any adults do in the privacy of their bedrooms is their own business, and any effort to criminalize their behavior is unconstitutional. After that ruling, I don't think you can find much of anything in Walt Whitman that would be a problem for mainstream Republicans. He was the singer of development, of manifest destiny, of men going to work and building cities. He's out there singing into existence the condominiums and shopping malls, the highways, the colorful throngs of people that flock into ballparks & museums or who eat at Burger King. He's celebrating NAFTA, WTO, and the production of countless high-tech gadgets.

I exaggerate. But I do think it time to put him reverently on the shelf alongside Milton and Petrarch, a model for poetic craft. He's almost *too much* the stenographer of consciousness.

Thoreau on the other hand has hardly been digested. He went to jail refusing to pay war taxes on an imperialist grab that Whitman was singing in praise of. It was his essay "Civil Disobedience" that gave Mahatma Gandhi his directive, and then through Gandhi, Martin Luther King, Jr. Comparatively few Americans have caught up with that mistrust of their government's policies, and that willingness to take a stand.

For North America, Thoreau was also the singer of responsible development. He watched the railroad being built & foresaw what it meant for forests, ecosystems, wildlife, and human populations. I bet in a shuddering dream he saw the automobile, the increasing addiction to fossil fuels, and a nation crisscrossed by asphalt highways that would hungrily displace animal migration routes. He devoted his life to a study of Native American lore, hoping to find a measured alternative to the headlong expansion of human settlement, a way to live on the planet lightly. His years at Walden Pond were an experiment to determine what a person actually, vitally required in order to survive. Thoreau became an active & outspoken Abolitionist. All the while he was reading Asian texts—Hindu, Buddhist, Taoist, tribal—and seeing them as more vital to this country than many of the head-trips of Europe.

And he was, importantly, not anti-technology. Most people don't know that he invented the modern pencil, the pencil as we grew up with it. Besides working in his family's pencil factory, he may have been the finest surveyor of his day. But he wanted a technology on the scale of what later visionaries—of the nineteen-sixties & seventies—hoped for: human in scale, with self-renewing energy sources. Almost nothing of his vision has been put into place; what little has crept through (like Emancipation, or the vote for women, or the Wilderness and Endangered Species Acts) has been brought forward by struggle, and still aren't firmly established. Thoreau is the "other" America, the one that hasn't come into existence yet.

TC: As a younger buck back east, did Kerouac or his companions register on your radar screen at all?

AS: Hardly. East coast establishment buried most of it. A few magazines like *Ramparts* could be had. I'd heard of Ginsberg and Ferlinghetti but knew only a book or two. The one poet of that crowd I read with great attention was LeRoi Jones (Amiri Baraka). Then just before I left New England I started to read Chinese poetry in translation. That was when I encountered Gary Snyder's *Cold Mountain Poems*. Those hit me, along with a lot of India material I was turning on to, and I went off to Asia. I was twenty. When I returned it was to California.

TC: You turn up in the S.F. Bay Area studying Sanskrit at university. That's uncommon enough to be worthy of attention. What event(s) stimulated this turn of mind?

AS: I'd been reading Hindu and Buddhist texts in translation for a long time and even tracked a little Sanskrit. I loved the thunder and hurtling winds, the surging mountains and voluptuous deities, the folkloric humor that comes in from Paleolithic backgrounds. A dear friend, Bhuwan Joshi, who had been raised in the Kathmandu Valley, helped me work through some *Upanishads* and he made the old poems come totally alive. So I kind of raided the University at Berkeley to learn Sanskrit, wanting to read deeply into those texts. I never did get a degree. It became clear that my motive was to learn how to read certain core books in the language, not become a professional. Bhuwan had encouraged me to study Sanskrit, and sadly he died the year I formally began at Berkeley. But in the sinews of the old language I began to find fantastic material for poetry—as he told me I would—as well as to witness a magical transformation of the old books.

TC: Was there any significant spiritual dimension in this Indic interest or was it more secular? A literary interest? Some combination? Had you grown up in New England with a sense of religion?

AS: I'm not sure I believe in these as separate dimensions any longer. At the time I would have said my interests were spiritual. I'd grown up with no religious allegiance whatever. My first contact with any meaningful sense of spiritual awe or ecstatic union came first through an early love, then through contact with some rugged backcountry. A sense of the spiritual came more formally through the sculpture of India and the ink paintings of China and Japan. I found these art works in the museums of Boston and Cambridge. They were images of consciousness for me—places I wanted to be, spiritually. Notice that in Indian sculpture religion and sexuality are often intertwined, as in China religion and wilderness are often inextricable.

Later as my confidence as a poet grew, and I realized the spiritual call of literary work, I began to search out India's poetry. But at the start I wanted to understand the kinds of things said in Buddhist sutras and Hindu texts, things that accorded with my own experience and instincts. Like many people, psychedelic drugs opened some doors, and the vast speculative mind spaces found in Asian texts were useful guides to what was going on.

TC: In your essay on William Everson we get a look into the development of your own mind at what appears to be a pivotal time in your career. Did he carry with him any of the old politics of his pacifist WW II years? Any of this rub off? How about the heavy influence of Jeffers on Everson: have you a sense that Jeffers still sings to people?

AS: Bill was a perfect example of Yeats' "Why should not old men be mad?" Here I take mad to mean something like "wild." Bill's politics, his pacifism, had been deeply etched into his dramatic life. The political stance rubbed off through simply being around him. Most of our friendship was based on a regard for craft not politics though. I worked with him on a letterpress book at the Lime Kiln Press and we looked over another of his projects, *American Bard*, together. We talked about women, love, the writings of Ananda Coomaraswamy, forest fires across the bay at Big Sur; and we sat quietly on the porch of his Kingfisher Flats cabin and smoked cigars. He was getting old, the Parkinson's disease was just becoming evident, so he was entering that ruminative phase that comes with advancing age. His wildness lay coiled up within him. The Whitman beard and hair, the wide brimmed hat, bear claw necklace, buckskins— these were like monk's robes to him. Outer evidence of his inward quest. I guess I'd have to say his politics were not organized or dogmatic or particularly articulated. They were the outcome of his religious discoveries, his struggle with Catholicism.

Jeffers was the master poet for Bill. In terms of West Coast poetry, and its effort to get the staggering land forms into verse, Jeffers remains the most powerful expression of what Bill called the Western archetype. I guess Jeffers still sings to people. Stanford has published his collected poetry in four huge expensive volumes, and recently brought out two volumes of selected poetry. He's got what Melville called the wild game flavor—like venison—lean and untamed. It won't be to everyone's taste. I have been writing a poetry sequence that wrestles with Jeffers, I try to lighten him up a bit, make some fun with his gloominess. Bill wrote much of his own poetry wrestling with Jeffers, and it was like a struggle of giants. Face to face Bill was a deeply humorous man, but in his poetry he has the crashing granite, terrifying Pacific coast storms, and sacramental violence Jeffers kept writing about. It's not a taste our urban, educated, professional classes have cultivated.

TC: Moving out of your acquaintance with Everson, your excellent essay on the continuing relevance of the small press tradition offers a furtherance of this attention to craft. You're involved yourself now in fostering this tradition at Naropa with students. Can we speak here a little about lineage? The notion of lineage-bearing looks to have slipped a point or two in western culture, although it would appear to be a core tenet at Naropa.

AS: You're right. The idea of lineage remains central to Naropa's Jack Kerouac School. Poetry is a weave of lineage with no time or place constraints. You may not meet masters in daily life, but that doesn't mean they aren't there instructing you.

Our postmodern condition is that each of us has our own lineage—individual and precise, instructive, full of direct transmissions of consciousness. I see a good poem as an emboided state of mind. At any moment you can slip right in, or through. The secular perspective says, "Well, he's self-taught. He's an autodidact. He didn't get it from anyone else. He found his voice." That's what the books say of Kenneth Rexroth for instance. I think that view is bullshit. The other side says: I have direct access to the mind of Aeshylus, to Sappho's mind, to the thoughts and ardor of the early Sanskrit poets, to Tu Fu, Shakespeare. Only the thinnest veil divides me from Lady Murasaki. "All times are contemporaneous in the mind," Ezra Pound wrote. When I read and translate the poems of Vidya or Lady Shilabhattarika in Sanskrit, I'm receiving direct transmission through the body of language.

"The body of language." That, by the way, is a term I learnt from Bhartrihari—he lived about eighth century India. "Body of language." He whispered it in my ear through a poem 1300 years ago.

TC: Let's talk linkages. Something brought you to the West Coast and kept you there for seventeen years. Something brought you to Colorado. We've touched upon some of the formative literary elements in your life back east, the centering experience of Sanskrit study, and your learning to work with fine press techniques. How was your development as a poet coming along? Were the various streams intertwined or have they necessarily run along parallel tracks? Inevitably, they seem to converge, but in terms of process were you obliged to compartmentalize different parts of your life?

AS: I was writing all along. It wasn't until my mid-twenties, though, that I realized how central the writing had become. It's a funny development. I had been supporting myself by work in a bakery—this was in the mid-seventies. I'd turned myself into a pretty good innovative baker, working in a California establishment with natural foods—whole-wheat flour, honey, organic butter—and decided to write a baking cookbook. I spent a lot of time in the library investigating the origins of baking. The more I worked at the cookbook, the more I found my real interest was not baking but writing—study and writing. When I saw this clearly the cookbook dropped along the wayside and I turned to poetry. I made the gesture of seeking out Bill Everson. It was a way of saying to myself, I'm a poet and I want to meet the lineage holders who are still alive. I want to know their minds. So I turned my love of craft from the bakery to the print shop.

Studying Sanskrit at first was a separate activity; I didn't know quite how it hooked up. When I stumbled upon the impossibly complex, elegant poetry tradition of classical India I began to see how the work of translation could be central to my commitment as a poet. Virtually nobody outside India knew Sanskrit poetry at the time, so I happened on it cold. By 1978, when I set out to study Sanskrit in earnest, well-read Americans knew Basho, Lady Murasaki, Tu Fu, Po Chu-i. No one had heard of Bhartrihari, Yogeshvara, King Hala, or Vidya. This was the best lesson I have ever learnt about poetry: the real work may lie where you aren't expecting it. The lesson is about accident, happenstance, synchronicity, magic. World folklore points this out time and time again. Sometimes I think of it this way, an image that came through a dream. The scholar goes out tracking his prey, knows its habits, where it wanders, uses skills precise as a hunter's, and brings the animal down. The poet releases his arrow but often misses his prey. He is obliged to plunge deeper into the forest in search of that arrow, and there finds the unexpected.

That's why I love the account of Kurt Schwitters' discovery of chance operation. Frustrated with one of his drawings because it looked so conventional, so boring, he tore his composition apart and tossed away the shreds in disgust. When he looked down he saw an unexpected beauty: a new configuration on the floor.

TC: Looking back, do you have a sense of how your poetry was coming along?

AS: I had to learn that lesson first. About chance, and about heartbreak. About missing the target. Then I had to learn about cut-up, bricolage, and the ideogramic method of Pound. It was slow learning. I had to learn how to think like the poets of ancient India so I wouldn't just repeat what had been done by Bill Everson. Or by Baraka or Niedecker or Snyder or any of the poets I admire. I had to speak everyday with dead poets—"all times are contemporaneous in the mind"—argue points of craft with them, fill up notebooks with ideas and words I had stolen. I had to figure out how to go forward with no preconceptions. This makes it sound close to Zen practice. Basho wrote, don't follow in the steps of the old masters, seek what they sought.

TC: The other chief informing element in your mature work is what I suppose we used to call "natural science." By this I mean there's been a progressive sharpening of attention to ecological detail in your work. There are times in Wild Form, Savage Grammar *where the narrative voice is so thoroughly imbued with place, with a kind of systems theory awareness of local ecological inventories that, in a deeply appreciative sense, we can practically hear Gary Snyder in there. Can you comment on this development in your work: was there a triggering moment for you when you decided to know the names of the birds and trees in your community terrain? What part of your living experience led to the kind of bioregional awareness that turns up in your letter to the government requesting that Christo's proposed eco-wrap project be directed elsewhere?*

AS: That's a personal and pretty complex question. How can I answer except by telling stories, or pulling together a few threads of thought? As I said, in California the mountains were my great teachers. In Colorado I do my apprenticeship with the Rockies. The eco-zones and watersheds are what I've come to love. It all happens in the details, so of course I learn what I can. "Details are the life of prose." That's Kerouac. The same for poetry. Same for ecology. Maybe I got my interest from too much time in Thoreau territory as a kid! I used to swim in Walden when it was forbidden and get chased off by rangers.

On a more sober note, the planet's ecosystems are now our neighborhood, our house, our home. Inside a home you give things the dignity of their names. I don't generally call my daughter or my girlfriend "hey you" or ask them to pass the whatsit. Names are powerful, full of magic. They call things otherwise unseen into existence. There is a politics in this too.

As for Christo's wrap of the Arkansas River, I don't want it directed somewhere else, I want it rejected because of its potential for hazard. If Christo wants to wrap something up in synthetic fabric, make it a building or a bridge or a refrigerator, not a fragile ecosystem. I'd be glad to walk the high country with him, check out a few plants and animals, and together we could talk about why sinking steel anchors into rock in bighorn sheep territory isn't a good idea.

TC: Given the state of the world this eco-mindedness is important, so let's develop it further. It seems pretty clear that writers from out of the Beat culture have had an outsized impact in fostering improved environmental awareness in our time. Is it a basic social justice/leftist/community-mindedness that may be inherent in the beat ethos that's helped spawn this? What aspects of beat culture would you say led to this form of awakening? Is it as simple, maybe, as there being a preponderance of beat poets who went camping with their folks when they were kids and had at least some basic forest/wilderness savvy, or is it deeper? Since the N.Y.C. contingent of Kerouac, Ginsberg, Burroughs et al were essentially, though not exclusively, urban (at least early days), were the west coast/S.F. Renaissance personalities key, the Oregon/Washington State band of Welch, Whalen, Snyder or . . .?

   American academic culture has had fits with the Beats, notably so with its ecologically-attuned dimensions. I'm thinking here of the old east coast put-down of Snyder's poetry as "the bear-shit on the trail school" (which of itself is a remark-ably perceptive epithet!). Nowadays it's not unheard of to hear Wendell Berry, Wes Jackson or Snyder and others brushed off as Neo-Luddites (which again can be seen as spot on). What is there in this form of put-down, do you think?

AS: These are big questions and I'm not an expert. But I think the emergence of an environmental movement, an ecologically sound approach to life and the arts, and the development of bioregional consciousness—these are huge matters of human consciousness. This is a critical and strangely exhilarating moment in human history. The chance to ruin or retrieve the planet as a viable sphere of life is in front of us. Do poets create these recognitions, these shifts in consciousness, or simply announce them? Or document them? Anyone paying a bit of attention recognizes that the Earth's amazingly resilient biosphere has met its match in contemporary human populations and technologies. With or without the poets, questions about clean air, clean water, chemical and nuclear contamination, vanishing wild life, compromised wild lands, and so forth, will be hugely debated.

At the moment the real leaders are not in the developed world. They are in India and Chiapas. What the beats did was to make issues like these appear in American poetry. They made poetry serious, bringing an activist approach to crisis, as Ezra Pound did by leveling his gaze at economics and war.

As for the put-down of poets, it always happens. There are many ways to make a poem, many things to write about, many sympathies and ideas to explore. Most of the celebrated poets of the past hundred years, and nearly all the academics and critics, have been urban dwellers. They want something else from a poem than bearshit on the trail. Fair enough. But if poets took put-downs too seriously we wouldn't have any durable poetry at all! What if Catullus had listened to those temperate citizens of Rome when they said, you can't write shit like that about love affairs and politics, someone might have you assassinated. What if Anna Akhmatova had listened to the Stalinist censors? Chaucer is very funny, dramatizing a big put-down of his skills in *The Canterbury Tale*: "your rhymes are not worth a turd." It's true. You and I could be out making real money, Trevor, not following this thankless path of poetry.

TC: The next obvious point crops up during your essay discussion about how certain American, particularly Pacific Northwest poets/translators, develop a yen for classical Chinese/Japanese aesthetics in art and poetry. This has tended to fit hand-in-glove with an interest in Buddhism and Taoism. As interest in Buddhism is undergoing a boom in the West do you have much sense that influence from Beat-affiliated writers continues to play a role in this? Have we reached a point where knowledge of the Dalai Lama, Thich Nhat Hanh, Chogyam Trungpa Rinpoche and others may have sufficiently mainstreamed that The Dharma Bums *isn't as central as it once was? Your professional experience at Naropa makes you uniquely qualified to address this point.*

AS: You couldn't imagine American poetry at present without the influence of Chinese and Japanese models. The work of many fine translators—translators who have undertaken the difficult study of one or more Asian languages, often old literary languages along with contemporary spoken ones—has rapidly altered how North Americans write poetry. Buddhist thought and practice are something else. These will need a longer timeframe in order to lay down durable foundations, and possibly they will require that temples, monastic settings, colleges, and other institutions survive for generations. The Buddhist teachers you mention are instrumental; there are many, many more, and quite a few effective ones with no celebrity recognition at all. It is lovely to have North America able to support Buddha halls where poets can come and go at will—like Tu Fu and Li Po did, Basho, Sei Shonagon. But thinking back to an era when few temples existed here, in the annals of American Buddhism the beat poets will necessarily figure as wily, savvy, quixotic buddha ancestors.

I hope one day everyone will see *The Dharma Bums* as a first great book of American Buddhist poetry. Let's imagine that for a thousand years it spurs readers to emulate the masters of the past: to write poetry, to practice zazen, to take vows of creativity and restraint. To study big Mind, to lock eyebrows with Bodhidharma and Han-shan, to drink tea with beloved companions. To head on foot into the mountains with a rucksack full of books. To cultivate visions, to practice love. *Dharma Bums* is a big brave book, which most American should read. It is full of pain and fuck-ups too, alcoholism, tragic affairs, and a suicide. So I have one word of caution about the beats. It's from Bashō. Don't follow in the footsteps of the masters; seek what they sought.

TC: Further to the links between poetry, ecology and Asia: you discuss the resurgent idea of cross-species empathy on the part of eco-activists and formally name it "jataka mind." It's a brilliant declaration. Can you summarize the understanding this represents?

AS: I drew the idea from a number of related studies in ecology, art, and psychology. The word *jataka* is Sanskrit; it means birth, or life, as in lifetime. The *Jataka Tales*, originally oral tales, eventually written down in Pali, are early Buddhist stories. In them the Buddha—long before he is born Prince Siddhartha—shows up in former lifetimes, most often in animal form. In each story he makes some extreme sacrifice, often to save the lives of critters of another species. Have you ever seen the rabbit in the moon? Go out and look closely at the full moon and you'll see the imprint of a rabbit. It's there because long ago the Buddha, living as a rabbit, couldn't bear the hunger of a group of unsuccessful, starving hunters. He jumped into their pot to feed them. To commemorate the act, one of the old gods, Indra, mightily impressed at the show of compassion, put that rabbit's image on the moon. "The hare-marked moon."

My essay simply observes that creatures of divergent species—including we *homo sapiens*—have an inherent empathy for one another. Buddhists are familiar with this, theoretically at least. So are Jains, Hindus, Taoists. Christians have charity, though many seem unsure what do with St. Francis when he extends his good will to non-human creatures. In our own day I see it most among people who get pegged as animal rights or ecology activists. I like to think that they are also pioneers towards a new spiritual sense of our place on this planet.

When I wrote my essay it was partly to celebrate the bravery of the Redwood Summer activists who were putting their lives on the line for old growth trees, spotted owls, salmon, the entire understory of the forests of the Northwest, and related eco-systems. I had not yet read Edward O. Wilson's Biophilia Hypothesis, which is a prop-osition by a respected scientist that matches the poetry speculations my essay got into. Wilson's sound biological ruminations are where I'd go next. From the standpoint of deep time—the point of view of evolution—all species are fellow travelers in complex ecosystems. Different animals aren't simply a colorfully benign costume for the planet that we humans get to groove on—or snuff out if they get in our way. Diverse species are intricately woven into our lives along metabolic, ecological, and spiritual pathways. We utterly depend on each other, not just for food and fertility, or clothing, but for companionship. It will be a very lonely planet for everyone when the last elephant has been hunted down for its ivory, or if we lose the grizzly bear and the wolf.

These creatures, as world folklore repeats again and again, are our sympathetic teachers. More than that, they make us. When you're wandering up a hiking trail and the buzzing of a small rattler's tail makes you leap backwards—that's because we have co-evolved. Our brain is structured the way it is partly because snake lives out there in the bush. Didn't snake provide us humans with coolly alert senses, able to note a slight quaver in the brush at our feet, able to leap aside without having to calculate? Snake gave us the skills we hone in the martial arts dojo. We owe much of our psycho-physical competence to Snake Old Man! So, recognizing and cultivating those old contracts of respect, admiration, companionship—this would be the hip, archaic, far-seeing, and lovely new way to be human. A rattlesnake isn't bad. It just wants respect. Not to be trod upon. It gives us a quick lesson, and then does its job of cleaning up the vermin, aerating the soil, and possibly leaving the poet with a crisp little song.

What I call Jataka Mind would be the deep-level recognition that these connec-tions exist, are ultimately important, and that in the large picture no one—no spe-cies—is dispensable. We have to take care of one another. This is a sensibility we can cultivate and pass on to friends and children. Studying ecology is one way in, medita-tion might nail a few things down, but stories and poems are the best way to celebrate interspecies kinship. Why do kids want to hear animal stories? Same reason that the early stories of every culture have animals showing up in them. Humans have been profoundly curious about other beings—they are our teachers—and it's reciprocated. Animals are helpers, assistants, companions. Some extend real friendship towards humans. They like us, you know. We're weird and interesting to them. They come around to check out the crazy things we cook up.

TC: A longish, compound query: In your essay "Notes on Form & Savage Mind" you remind us that the essential patterns of nature constitute "a far-reaching grammar"—to paraphrase Chuang-tzu, one that picks up where words leave off. Later (bottom of p. 82), you note that "Dream like evolutionary theory predicates shapeshifts and transformations." Shapeshifting is a recurrent theme in the bardic tales of the old Celts—psychologists have a field day with Cuchulain's adversaries becoming scary monsters, what have you. I note occasional Celtic references in your book. Perhaps as a bridge here, we could point to your interest in interglacial age cave-art where the shaman-artist seems to serve an intermediary role in striking connections between "wilderness/wild mind" and, say, dream. And if it's not too far a reach, in your Indian ventures you've observed sadhus as envoys of this eternal-moment Deamtime here and now. Interestingly, you dedicate this key essay to poets Robin Blaser and Joanne Kyger. Blaser, of course, has affiliation with the Robert Duncan-Jack Spicer stream, and Kyger with her own manifold poetic linkages.

AS: I love it that ecology is scientifically confirming what poetry, dream, and stories always told us. Things change, people change, landscapes change, everything shapeshifts in meaningful and sometimes unpredictable ways. In the old time, animals were people and people animals. No paleontologist has ever found an indication of anything else. All living creatures are on complicated journeys from form to form, and the postmodern poem has to deal with it. The postmodern mind has to deal with it.

Celtic material is something I've just started to dig into. You know, it is very, very close to the old stuff I find in India. Like I say in a poem, "Banaras to Dublin to

Boston, it's an Indo-European thing." Here I'm thinking about language per se, and the grand playful shifts that happen through time. I recently went on an exploration of the Aran Islands off Ireland's west coast—looking for old tombs, forts, hermit hutches, holy wells, and other sites. I used Tim Robinson's good, detailed map, and read his two-volume *The Stones of Aran*. His work shows how in Ireland every rock, every little inlet or old tree, each cliff face or rock outcrop, has a name. Every name has a story, and every story has a history or legend. It's like going on a nature walk with a good biologist—in six hours you might not get past the weed-lot twenty feet from the classroom door. I mean if he's a *good* biologist.

Some of my poetry gets into this for Colorado. One poem I did with Althea, my daughter—she was about ten—we pulled out a Colorado gazetteer of place names. The poem includes a list: "A town called Gothic. A town called Troublesome. A canyon called Chaos. A rock called Elk Tooth." We were laughing and rolling around with the map. Talk about "a far reaching grammar!" She was a little shamaness of place names: "A town called McCoy. A gulch called Skeleton. A peak called Quandary. A town called Rifle. A park called Interlocken. A peak called Thunderbolt." The poem ends, "a bar called Rocky Flats."

TC: Thinking specifically of your poetry, there's an abundance of erotic imagery in your work. Is this organically Schelling or might it arise from your compelling interest in Sanskrit poetry wherein ripeness and fecundity often verge on carnality? Is there a special gift the Sanskrit offers our time?

Erotic energy is the energy of the planet. It is playful, loving, polymorphous, it is also dark, brooding, fecund, vegetative. The tricky thing for a poet in Western civilization is to find a language that can express this range. I don't need to go into the history of it, but for a long, long time in the West the language of sexuality was in the hands of the medical doctor or left out in the street. We don't have a tender, literary vocabulary for erotic love. It has been hard to depict love with lightness or vulnerability. What McClure and Lenore Kandel did, and writers like Joyce, Lawrence, Gertrude Stein before them, was very brave.

So a special gift left us, among others, by the Sanskrit poets of a millennium or two ago: erotic poetry that gets the lightness, the juice, the passion, the special human ways of courtship and consummation. You find it in Sappho and the other early Greeks too. But in old India the "language of love" was entrusted to the poets. In King Hala's *Sattasai*, a nearly 2000 year old anthology, an opening verse criticizes anyone who would claim to know something about love without reading poetry. Poetry is where you go to learn this stuff. It was commendable to study love in those days. Somewhere Kenneth Rexroth writes that in Sappho's culture the pursuit of sexual pleasure was totally respectable, the way making money is in our culture. I know where I'd like to live. What about you? A world where the discoveries of love define our lives? Or where the NASDAQ Index does?

TC: In "Allen Ginsberg Death Notes" you observe, "Dour white Protestant America needed a touch of music and ecstasy, and Allen helped bring that." You were privileged to work with Allen for many years at Naropa. What was it like to be in his presence over an extended period of time? Did you sense any deep dichotomies between the public and the private man? Was he comfortable in solitude or did he generally prefer to be among the company of others?

AS: I knew Allen from about 1990 until his death. Hundreds of people knew him much better than I did. He put up with me in a way that was sometimes grumbling, sometimes sweet natured. But I did get to see him in ways that he's not generally portrayed—sitting through long tasking administrative meetings, designing curricula for a writing program, or brainstorming ways to raise funds for Naropa. He had a good head for that kind of thing. He took it seriously. Our relationship was mostly built on practical jobs. We did teach or perform together at a number of poetry programs over the years. I don't think he cared too much for my poetry.

I also knew him in the waning years of his life. He had a lot of ailments and had to treat his aging body with enormous care. Special diets, lots of macrobiotic food, probably heaps of medication, insulin, chairs that didn't hurt his creaky back. I don't think his thirst for public life, or simply the presence of other people, ever dropped off though. A lot of folk loved him deeply, and he cared for so many! Underneath I always sensed something sadly far-off or alone. Bluesy.

My essay on him was not about any special intimacy. I just thought my Sanskrit studies, and conversations with him about that kind of thing, haiku and Buddhist practice, had generated a few curious anecdotes that people who weren't there might enjoy.

TC: As to Naropa and Kerouac School—one essay mentions Harry Smith with The Grateful Dead in the same breath, a lovely little parable. A very tender photograph of Harry appears in Allen Ginsberg's photography edition, Snapshot Poetics. *How are these three linked?*

AS: Harry was an old friend of Allen's. Allen brought him to Naropa—the story is he found Harry nearly dead in the Chelsea Hotel, cleaned him up—and Harry Smith lived his final years in a tiny clapboard building on our Arapahoe Street campus. He was there when I arrived, a kind of obscure elderly Dada coyote. He always had a gentle cult of students who were terribly loyal, and he was fun to seek out and talk to. He was like an oracle, I mean he didn't talk the way anyone else did. You'd say something and he'd come up with a kind of impenetrable aphorism. You'd say something else and he'd come out with another weird speech object. Conversation with him was like making a mosaic out of found objects.

Harry had put together the important *Anthology of American Folk Music* in the fifties, from which the big generation of rock 'n roll people learnt traditional American music. Blues, Appalachian fiddle, work songs, ballads, hollers, all that great vernacular shit. So someone got the Rex Foundation—the Grateful Dead's benevolent society—

to put up some money to keep Harry alive. Rent, food, a little bit, you know, some grass, a lot of books.

TC: Writing schools are a new growth area for academia. There's controversy about this, but the proof does seem to be there in the surprisingly talented graduates who are emerging. Canadian literature, at least, is the richer for them. If it doesn't sound naïve, how do you view the role of Naropa's celebrated Kerouac School these days? Has there been any change in operative mood since Allen's passing?

AS: It changes all the time! Because poetry changes. Some people were nervous when Allen died. "Uh-oh, that's it, how will the school continue? Allen is dead." But you know, it ain't a school, a University—a serious place of study and work—if it's dependent on the personality of one figure. That would be a cult. If it's a real place, with energy and vision, and accomplished faculty, and brilliant courageous students, it ought to get along simply because poetry is a craft that requires solid training. You can train alone, or you can train with other people. If you want to train with other people, a school is a noble place to do it.

The Writing office keeps a list of accomplishments by students—mostly books, but also grants, gigs, service, reputations, an impressive list. I can't tell you how edifying it is to read the Chinese translations of Mike O'Connor, or Shin Yu Pai's excellent new book of poems, or the non-stop magazines and journals and chapbooks begged or borrowed or stolen into print by students. The letter-press print shop, which we named for Harry Smith—man, you can't keep up with the beautiful items it produces: broadsides, chapbooks, postcards, book-art objects, odd little collaborative accordion poetry things.

TC: As someone on the ground at the Jack Kerouac School you've witnessed encounters with a phenomenal plurality of poetic and creative personalities, from the Beats, the New York and San Francisco schools, and major jazz and visual artists, through to language poets and religious masters. The lot. Are there some pinnacle moments or encounters with particular individuals from this rich, unfolding tapestry you can share?

AS: My philosophy—that's not the right word—my instinct—that's better—in my gut I regard poetry as a communal effort. Language is communal. It is made by hundreds, thousands, millions. Some are known people who got famous, many are quiet, hardly heard of, but every one indispensable. There is a huge psycho-conspiracy in this country, wrapped up in scandalous ways of making money, which pretends that the world is populated by a few geniuses, and the rest of the population is there to be inspired, exhilarated, thrilled, or instructed by these heroes. Namely, to pay for tickets to events, buy big selling books, consume CDs & celebrity magazines, whatever. I find this attitude ugly, stupid, reactionary, and infuriating. The only revolution will involve everyone when it arrives, not just the media stars. Marx saw this. Plants and animals included! I don't think Marx saw that. But the children do.

Hundreds of memorable people have come through Naropa, the roll going far deeper than the big names. Much of it has been audio or video taped, and there's a large archives project in place now, with help from the NEA and elsewhere, to get this material secured, digitalized, made available. Remove a single visitor from the archive and the archive ecology is violated.

Okay, having given my rant, I can quiet down and mention a few notable moments. Hearing Carl Rakosi in his nineties engage in deep gossip about the Objectivists one hot afternoon was a high point. He told how he made the long trip out to Black Hawk Island, Wisconsin, to visit Lorine Niedecker. He'd never met her in person. She said, "Louis Zukovsky is the greatest living poet, isn't he?" Carl said no, I don't see it that way, and went out and spent the afternoon painting the shed with Lorine's husband Al, or something like that.

Meeting Miriam Patchen and watching her deflect any suggestion that she might have been partly responsible for her husband's poetry, was a high point. I found her fearless, acid tongued, bitingly humorous. We met a few times, wrote to each other, and had a funny relationship. She'd see me and start right in—"You can't be a poet if you're in a classroom! How can you waste yourself like that?" She'd write me, "Schelling, are you still in that class room? You'll kill any poetry in you." That kind of thing. It kept me on my toes. I really loved her. Then her house in Palo Alto got wiped out in a flood and she died shortly after.

Any one of Lorenzo Thomas's lectures on the blues, on racial identity, on whatever. To hear him chuckle with rich good-natured humor. Joanne Kyger never stops surprising me with her wild syntax and dry eco-humor, and I hope Harryette Mullen will keep her thing going for decades. One precious event I don't think got onto tape was about 1989: Gary Snyder and Peter Warshall debating the Endangered Species Act, with Gary taking the part of the ranchers and loggers. Most ecology activists were pretty myopic in those years. Like, "Bring in the ranchers and see what they want? Fuck that." So Gary took the rancher-logger side. I bet he converted a few people that day. He was not just rooting into his upbringing in the Pacific Northwest, but seeing the seed of the future. Because the ranchers, the loggers, the salmon fishers, have been here a long time and aren't going to just go away.

I remember that debate, because ten years later I had to organize a crew to shut down plans to construct a telecommunication tower near Trout Creek Pass in central Colorado. An international conglomerate, which puts up cell phone towers in sixty countries, was going to wreck some good high-altitude forest territory with a poorly thought out construction that violated zoning ordinances. They tried to play up the scary side of no cell phones: what happens if your grandchild has an accident and there is no cell phone service. Guess who we had on our side—this was 2001—in front of the Board of Adjusters in Fairplay? A rancher, a retired military officer, an accountant, a fieldworker for the U.S. Geological Survey. The rancher hated those towers, they were going up on all the ridges around Park County. He pulled out studies and testified that half the towers were there not to deliver signals, but to block service from rival companies!

Like Whitman said, "The United States are themselves the greatest poem."

TC: And a last question. The literary sensibility is perennial, but from the mixing of Eastern and Western literary/creative/aesthetic traditions, do you intuit any specific school or wave evolving out of this cross-pollinating intelligence? Something that might in part be heir to the Beats, as they acknowledged others before them—Imagists, Symbolists, Pound, Lawrence, Baudelaire—a kind of "new world dharma" perhaps?

AS: New World dharma! I love that. It would be the hip side of Globalism wouldn't it? I just don't want to lose the local though. I mean the details. I hope we can reverse the trend of animal and plant species extinction; also language and poetry tradition extinction. So I think—if we're lucky—we'll head into a poetry that is conversant in many, many languages. And that people will wake up and start translating like crazy.

When I went to Mexico City in 1994 I visited with a number of poets including Elsa Cross and David Huerta. Hearing them talk I realized, *they know all the USA poets!* Up here in El Norte we read or know of hardly anyone south of the Alamo. Octavio Paz. Who else?[1] That's why I designed a Translation Concentration for the Kerouac School. I'd have to say, if you're going to be a poet of the future, learn another language. Translate. Ezra Pound said in *The Cantos*, "It can't all be in one language." What I'm talking about is committed, long-term conversation between traditions. Who can discuss these things in Basque? Hopi? Gaelic?

I'd like to see dharma in there too, but not as a standardized religion or set of poetry protocols. Religion makes me anxious, ever since 1993 when I went to India and the adherents of three religions were slaughtering each other. So just to suggest a few values: human intelligence, cross-species compassion, some wise elderly women who remember what it all means, wine, song, wilderness, confident children. Maybe a Buddhist economics of simplicity or restraint, like E.F. Schumacher imagined several decades ago, but such a thing looks like it's way off in the future.

Meanwhile, give poetry room to play, lots of leeway to make up the future. There are so many different ways to make a poem, so many reasons, and the more range the better.

But young poets will have to give up the idea that it's a good career move. We should shut down the big publishing house dinosaurs and celebrate that a thousand small presses have bloomed. Another thing Pound said: "Poets are the antennae of the race."

The race as always is between the tortoise and the hare.

1. Ten years ago when Trevor Carolan and I spoke, this was the case. Quite a lot of back-and-forth translation has happened since, and several substantial anthologies of Mexican poetry came into print. Meanwhile, Roberto Tejada and Kristin Dykstra's journal *Mandorla*, a kind of yearly anthology, does a good job of bridging English-Spanish or North-South borders, and brings in a lot of Cuban poets too.

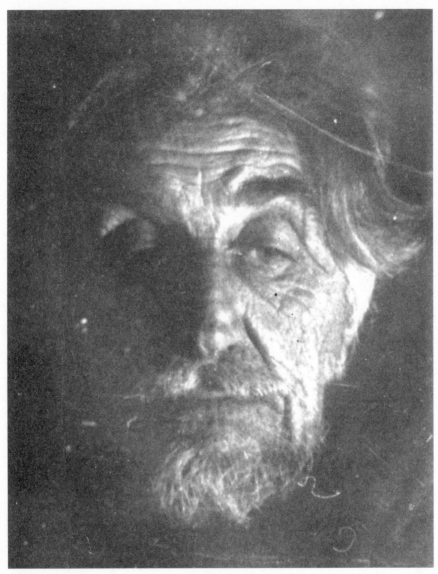

Jaime de Angulo, ca. 1949-1950

The Songs of Jaime de Angulo

Listen, this is my song. Remember that song. When you want me,
you come here and sing my song. I'll hear you. I'll come.
"Songs of the Indians of Northern California"

The great cultural region that makes up Northern California is the habitat of Jaime de Angulo's poetry. In the south there are the ocean-breasting granite cliffs, steeply pitched redwood forests, and plunging canyados of Big Sur. Far to the northeast lies the dry sagebrush plateau of Alturas. If you knew nothing of Jaime you could calculate precise quadrants for these poems, based on who shows up in them. Fox and coyote. Bluejay, wildcat, mountain lion, vulture. If these don't instantly conjure the Coast Range mountains and a series of landscapes within a day's drive of San Francisco, then the native vegetation will. Redwood, pine, poppy. Even the introduced plants say California: eucalyptus, jonquil, bamboo, almond tree. As I read through de Angulo's songs and poems again, I notice the density of wildlife. So many songs for deer, bullsnake, raven, hawk, quail, lizard, junco, beetle, frog, duck, locust, dragonfly, or raccoon.

Sometime during the late 1970s in Berkeley a friend put in my hands a copy of de Angulo's novella *The Lariat*. It is volume five of seven in the Jaime de Angulo Library, handsomely published by Bob Callahan's Turtle Island Foundation. I began reading de Angulo avidly, tracking down hard to locate monographs of anthropology or linguistics. I scoured archives in the Special Collections rooms of libraries at U.C. Santa Cruz and Berkeley. When several years later I attempted to qualify for an English MA degree at U.C. Berkeley, I proposed a thesis on the work of Jaime de Angulo. Not one of six professors I approached would sponsor me. After a dispiriting exchange with a Department staff member over whether de Angulo was worth an academic study, I quit school & did not return. One irony is that the same University had in the late twenties distanced itself from de Angulo, refusing him help with a unique collection of California Indian song he had recorded on wax cylinders, which were in danger of disintegrating. The anthropologists didn't want him then, the English professors rejected him fifty years later.

But that's partly what makes Jaime de Angulo so distinct. Outside any official channel of recognition or tribute he has become an outsize figure in small communities and backwoods camps of Northern California. A figure of folklore. East of the Sierra Nevada his books also pass hand to hand. It's in California, though, that dog-eared copies of *Indian Tales* are fixtures in households—like chainsaws, work gloves, automobile parts. Over the years I have collected a medicine pouch of stories about Jaime, often from people met by chance in Nevada County, in Arcata, around Berkeley, or in the hills and inns of Big Sur.

A landmark of the search into de Angulo's writings came in the mid-nineties when a book dealer from Northern California came up with an item listed as "Collected Poems of Jaime de Angulo." I bought the manuscript: soft yellowing photocopy paper in a hunter's green binding. Many of its poems were new to me. Where the manuscript originated I have no idea. The copies are of a typewriter font I know as de Angulo's. There are many pages, grainy from archaic copy machines, in his hand. Sometimes corrections, drawings or doodles, inscriptions, dates, or a signature. A number of full poems. It appears that before his death in 1950 Jaime had considered a book like the present one. The old manuscript opens with "Shaman Songs," continues with Lorca translations, and concludes with "Songs of the Hillside," first and second choices.

"Shaman Songs." De Angulo must have regarded many of these poems as power objects not literary pieces. He drew his "songs" from decades of friendship with members of the Achumawi, Pomo, Karok, Modoc, and Miwok tribes. His daughter

Gui writes that for most of his life Jaime avoided poetry. Especially the dressed-up European type, which would have violated his West Coast temper.

> I wrote a sonnet,
> And obeyed all the rules,
> Of tercets and quatrains, and
> In fourteen lines I finished it all
> So smoothly.
> And still my heart was uncertain.

Along with distinct plants, animal life, landforms, and weather patterns, California is home to a rich cultural tradition of story, and a confounding stock of native languages. Behind a wood stove I keep on the wall John Wesley Powell's celebrated map, "Linguistic Stocks of American Indians North of Mexico," first published in 1888. Great single-color swathes cover millions of square miles across present-day Alaska, Canada, the Great Plains and Great Basin. In these territories, dominating the map, languages of four linguistic families were spoken: Algonkian, Athapascan, Siouxan, and Shoshonean. By contrast the West Coast is a patchwork of bright tiny colors, each outlining the territory of a separate language stock. Indians and anthropologists have determined that over 100 languages were spoken in California in precontact days. Fifty still have currency.

Jaime knew this world better than anyone else of his day.[1] Even Alfred Kroeber, doyen of California anthropology in its Golden Age, author of a hundred treatises on the Indians, and a kind of nemesis of Jaime's, knew it less well. He lacked Jaime's skill for language, he lacked Jaime's freedom as an unaffiliated scholar; more importantly, he lacked Jaime's reckless love for people & for experience. De Angulo received over the course of a dozen years more grants from Franz Boas's Committee on Research in Native American Languages than anyone. His job was to go into the field, find speakers of a tongue not yet described, make friends, write down in notebooks the language itself (all of them languages without writing systems); then to return to Berkeley or to his ranch on Big Sur's Partington Ridge and write them up. Some of his field studies have been published, many remain in manuscript only.

On one side, Jaime was a crackshot linguist. According to Edward Sapir and other specialists, his ear was better than anyone's. ("I dream of phonetics and passive verbs and modes and tenses all night long—it's as bad as working twenty-four hours a day.") On the other side, he had an instinct for people. He could befriend the wise, the circumspect, the perspicacious doctor, the brooding coyote—the person who could tell him the most. He could walk into a camp, sit in the shadows, sing songs picked up in other camps, and attach himself in a few days to someone whose friendship would hold for years. Someone who would prove unusually adept with language. Who knew the Old Time Stories & could sing the songs.

What intrigued him was how language disclosed the primitive mind. A mind, he contends, that can do everything with logic a modern civilized person would. But at the same time can cover other terrain—places of power, of magic, the old ways. Jaime wrote Cary Fink, his first wife, about William Benson, Pomo basket maker & story-teller—

> ... a remarkable fellow who is just as interested in glottal catches as
> I am. We spend hours looking into each other's throats with mir-
> rors and analyzing words and the rest of the cosmos just simply
> drops out ... he has invented a theory of having two souls, one
> that keeps the body alive and dies with the body, and the other, that
> never dies, but goes-a-wandering where you have lived, just as it
> does during sleep. And he proves it by arguments derived from the
> velocity of light! In one breath he talks about sugar in diabetes (his
> wife has diabetes) and in the next he speaks of symbolic magic (he
> believes it, too). I call him uncle and he calls me nephew.

De Angulo wrote a number of times about the songs of Northern California, highlighting the shaman songs ("Synonyms: medicine-songs; doctor-songs"). Among the Achumawi—the tribe Jaime felt closest to—shaman songs were an obsession. These were given to a person from "that world of mysterious beings who people Nature, but who, also, have wild and timid characters." Generally an animal power.

"Power, power, power, this is the burden of the song of everyday life," Jaime wrote in his early essay "The Religious Feeling in a Primitive Tribe." The major quest in primitive religion, he observed, was the search for some being who could deliver or convey to you a compressed form of the power that flows through all life. A person goes looking for "his power, his protector, his luck, his medicine, or whatever may be the English word preferred by any individual Indian." In the Achumawi tongue, this is your *dinihowi* (for regular people) or your *dama'agome* (for doctors or shamans).

The way you find a medicine is by *wandering*—going into the wilderness, losing yourself there, staying away from people, starving yourself, putting yourself in danger. Then,

> ... there is somewhere in the woods some individual animal, some one particular deer, or a certain locust, or a certain weasel, some one individual denizen of the wilds with a particularly strong dose of life-power to his credit, and he is the fellow whose acquaintance you must make and whose friendship you must acquire, cultivate, and keep. Go into the woods and find him. Seek him in the lonely places, about the springs. Call to him. Go again. Starve yourself and go again. Call to him. Sing his song. Try this song, try that song. Maybe he used to be somebody else's protector, somebody who died, and now he hears that song and he says: "That's my brother's song..."

In "The Music of the Indians of Northern California," first published in French in 1931, de Angulo calls out in the voice of a *dinihowi*. "Hey there! What are you doing here! You are singing a song that pleases me. It's *my* song. I'm going to give you my power. Go back to your home. Your family is worrying. I will take care of you. But you take care of me too. Come back and see me here, and sing my song. I will hear it and come." In the essay Jaime gives lines from four shaman songs. All four occur in this book.

Next to the restless poem on the sonnet I quoted above, the California manuscript holds this—

> I never was a man.
> I kill men.
> In the shadow of the bush I kill men.
> I the panther who never was a man.
> I the panther will come tonight.

·

In 1916, five years before de Angulo began formal anthropological fieldwork— he was twenty-nine years old—he went down the Big Sur coastline from Carmel. His guide was a vaquero who'd lost a thumb to *la reata* (the lariat) when it had wrapt around his saddle horn. Locally he was known as El Mocho—"lopped" or "chopped off." Finding a country wilder than any he'd experienced before—and only a day's trip by horse and stage back up the coast to friends in Carmel—Jaime homesteaded a piece of land high over the ocean. He named it Los Pesares, the Sorrows. It was his wilderness home. From that point on he divided his home-time between Los Pesares and a house in the Berkeley hills.

De Angulo pursued a restlessly productive career in linguistics and anthropology from 1921-1933. He "wrote up" seventeen languages from Northern California, including Achumawi, Karok, Shasta, Pomo, and did the same for nine Mexican languages.

He worked on Chinese, drawing up with his wife Lucy Freeland the Cantonese dialect. Some say he translated Lao Tzu, though as far as I've heard no manuscript has surfaced. He wrote four novellas during these years. (Side trips to Taos brought him into the the Mabel Dodge Luhan circle and a tempestuous acquaintance with D.H. Lawrence.) A few poems carry dates from this period, but the indication is most of his poems were written much later—if *written* is the proper term.

Things changed abruptly after a dozen years of linguistic field research. One afternoon in the summer of 1933, Jaime, his family, and a party of friends left Los Pesares with a small group of cars to drive the coast. The automobile Jaime and his son Alvar were riding in went over the cliff into Torres Canyon and fell a hundred and eighty feet—down through the redwoods before hitting the creek. Ten year old Alvar was killed and Jaime lay eleven hours in the wreck, before the car's driver managed to pry herself free and flag down a passing motorist. Jaime broke a leg and a shoulder. One apocryphal story says his body pinned down his son's those eleven hours, and his own rib went through Alvar's heart.

It took a lot of time—morphine and alcohol—for Jaime to recover physically. Psychologically the accident stayed with him. He plunged into depressions. It ended his active period of fieldwork. He struggled from then on with despairs. A madness came over, that in the biographies sounds Lear-like.

Several scholars have written that his turn towards literature occurred at this point—the point at which voices, voices other than the professional linguist's, begin to enter his writing. The point at which he loses his heart for fieldwork and withdraws to his Big Sur ranch, at first with his wife and daughter, later alone with a few stray field hands. Yet the appearance of voices in his writing was not new. In the 1926 article "Religious Feeling in a Primitive Tribe," after he describes the hunt for an animal protector—"Go into the woods and find him. Seek him in the lonely places, about the springs. Call to him. Go again. Starve yourself and go again. Call to him. Sing his song. Try this song, try that song,"—Jaime makes a curious move.

I have unintentionally dropped into the manner of speech of my
Pit River friends. What I have just said is not a quotation from any
one man but a sort of composite picture of what I have heard from
many.

This "unintentionally dropped into the manner of speech" is not just an innocent
aside. I don't think he inserts the phrase to protect himself from professionals who
want a more precise ethnography. It is the clue to *Indian Tales*, his finest work, and to
these poems. You find instances throughout his essays. It is the principle reason his
more sober colleagues thought him unreliable, a "variable personality" (Kroeber), dis-
reputable, troubling. De Angulo put it this way, in a footnote: "Decent anthropologists
don't associate with drunkards who go rolling in ditches with shamans."

A variation on the same theme. Jean Greensfelder showed up as a young woman
at Los Pesares during World War II. She published a brief recollection of de Angulo
decades later. In her account Jaime's hair and beard have grown out, he keeps a fire in
the living room with smoke hole knocked in the ceiling, and he is severely addicted to
alcohol. He arrives at the ranch from town with a case of rum, and brings one or two
bottles into the house. The others he assiduously conceals from himself out on the
rough, steep, brush covered hillside. At night she hears him out in the brush singing to
his rum bottles—"Gawd daaamn—where are you? Come to meee."

When I think of Jean's story I shudder. It is too close to Jaime's accounts of the
Achumawi doctors, singing in the brush for their medicines: "Raven, you, my poison.
COME."

I wrote that Jaime's finest work is *Indian Tales*. It's the place to best hear him drop
into those manners of speech of his Pit River friends. I don't mean the book, *Indian
Tales*, though it is awfully good and I brought my daughter up on it. I mean the series
of recordings he did the final year of his life for Pacifica Radio's KPFA in Berkeley.
These periodically get rebroadcast, and have been edited by de Angulo's daughter Gui
into eighty-eight sessions on twenty-two cassette tapes. On these you can hear many

of the songs in this book, in their strange, compelling English versions, as well as sung—repeatedly—in Pomo, Achumawi, or Western Miwok originals. Jaime's voice is irresistible, with its backdrop of Spanish, Basque, and French, and his peerless ear for tonality in Achumawi, whispers in Shasta.

A spooky set of tapes—full of voices, ghost voices. I mean there are voices whispering or singing in languages that no longer have living speakers.

You also hear a huge amount left out of the book. I would guess about a quarter of what's on the *Old Time Stories* tapes got into *Indian Tales* when edited by the publisher A.A. Wyn. "Most of the myths, virtually all of the songs, and the majority of the ethnographic data were omitted, as well as perhaps a third of the fictional narrative," notes the anthropologist Wendy Leeds-Hurwitz, who wrote her dissertation on de Angulo.

What Leeds-Hurvitz means by ethnographic data is stuff that sends shivers across your hide. Names of people, of animals, of plants; place names, articles of dress, tools—all in vocabularies of extraordinary precision—languages no longer extant in California. The tapes hold accounts of how to make a bow of yew and deer sinew, how to dress an elk, build a ceremonial longhouse, or work your way down a particular California drainage. Descriptions of puberty dances, of the mysterious Kuksu ceremony, of war skirmishes. Through it all, like the autumn song of the cricket: stories and songs that made their way around Northern California for thousands, maybe ten thousand, years. This is the real history of California.

I have been to Los Pesares, climbed to the ridgeline on the elusive Jaime de Angulo Trail, and scouted the campsite named for El Mocho. I have talked to neighbors who knew him, interviewed poets and Roman Catholics who tell cycles of stories about him, and scoured manuscripts and letters in the libraries. I want to tell you that his *Old Time Stories* manuscripts—the ones he prepared, as he was dying of cancer, to read over the radio—are disquieting & marvelous. They are written in a phonetic ("fonetik") script. Jaime had spent years recording languages in notebooks, out in the field, as they sounded. To the end of his life he wanted English simplified in its written

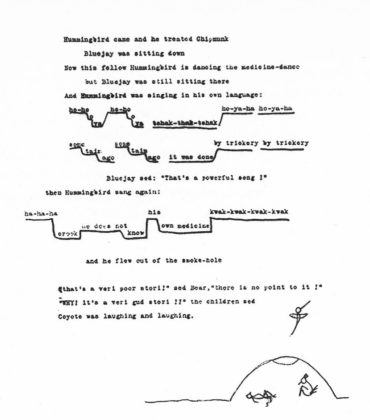

Manuscript page from Jaime de Angulo, "Indian Tales for a Little Boy and Girl"

form, so you could write it as it is spoken. He saw children wrestling with a crazy obsolete spelling system. He figured that could wreck a good mind.

Jaime's training in the field—and it was self training—was to go out, find a language that had never been recorded, and using some form of fonetiks take it down. As he heard it. At Kroeber's urging in the twenties he had learnt to record what the anthropologists called "texts": autobiography, conversation, description, song. And "myths": the old time stories.

Looking over Jaime's *Old Time Stories* manuscripts, with their eccentric spelling and linguist's symbols, I have the sensation that he is not writing the ordinary way. He is a listener passing on stories picked up on the trail or around the campfire. He is a storyteller, and a skilled linguist—simultaneously—passing along the myth as he hears it. I think his poems—his songs of the hillside, his shaman songs—came the same way.

In his writings on Indian song, Jaime had classified the types he found among Californians. First are the shaman songs, all of which he says contain words. Then gambling songs which do not have words. Jaime sees these as very old, left over from times when the languages were different. There are hunting songs, though these are disappearing—"In our day, with the rifle, naturally there is no more need for magical powers in order to kill the game!" War songs (also vanishing), animal songs, love songs, and dance songs. (These last being lost with the suppression of Indian dancing, but coming back a bit in our own day.) The animal songs ("every animal has its own special song") seem to be largely the same as shaman songs—"It's these songs here that the young people in search of supernatural power go off in the solitary wilds to sing."

The traditional shaman songs, the animal songs (and the fewer but similar plant songs) clearly are not made up by people, much less "written." If anything they are simply "written down." This is what I meant when I say they are objects of power not literary contrivances. They do not, after all, belong in an English department.

•

Describing events in other than chronological order is a Karok literary technique.
Jaime de Angulo

After twenty years in Northern California I now live along the eastern slope of the Southern Rocky Mountains. It is nowhere as thick & storied a region for poetry as those landscapes within a day's drive of the San Francisco Bay. The rough high-altitude frontier terrain of Colorado still spurs everyone into a raw, restless way of thinking. Even the literary people. Writers mostly visit. The ones that live here long-term have had to carry in their ideas of poetry on their backs, brought from elsewhere. This will change. It will be the land that changes it.

But for now I consider the Bay Area my poetry homeland—an increasingly distant Old Country, with particular customs and ways of thinking not prominent elsewhere. That part of the West managed to produce, in a stunningly short period, not only a lot of fine poetry to gladden the heart & keep the mind sharp. It also evolved a literature like that of no other place in the world, rooted in its bioregion. So I want to identify what to my thought are some characteristics of California poetry. Jaime de Angulo's influence on these qualities of perception will in years to come seem of enormous importance. A "distant influence," in Gary Snyder's words, for Gary's generation. For more recent generations, the story cycles that place Jaime and his colorful activities at their center may seem farther off—but his books fit closer to hand.

There is the centrality of wilderness. A rough, heartbreakingly lovely land, Northern California, even with timber, mining, agriculture, and other forms of high impact industrial change. Bill Everson wrote, "This land, like all beautiful places, crying out for tragedy." He was thinking of Robinson Jeffers, but it was Jeffers' close friend Jaime de Angulo who wrote in a letter, "I gnawed and ransacked my soul in this wilderness, alone with the fox, the rain, failure and insomnia." De Angulo's encounter with West Coast wilderness carries a weight of self-reliance that increases his influence every year. Drive the coast highway through Big Sur, get back into the foggy redwoods or stare out over the Pacific far below the granite cliffs. You'll see the land that Jaime's writings have scored, and a hunger for his books will gnaw at you.

There is also in California the non-negotiable presence of Asia. If you sweep your vision in a large northwards arc, you see that Native California sits on the Pacific Rim, and life for ten thousand years or more has been very similar, along this coast, to that in Beringia, coastal Siberia, Japan, Korea, China, and parts of Southeast Asia. Salmon & bear, tools for fishing & hunting, a repertoire of song, prayer, & joke. This means the turn to Native California, or the turn to Asia, for poets & scholars are not entirely different. In historic times with migration comes a distinct layering of residents: Native people with their hundred or more languages, then Spanish, Anglo, Chinese, Japanese. A mix of cultures and languages has been part of West Coast literature from the start. Robert Hass's Addison Street Poetry Project in Berkeley—bronze plaques of poetry native to the San Franisco Bay Area laid into the sidewalk—begins with Ohlone songs, a Yana song, poems by an anonymous Chinese immigrant, a Spanish woman, a Japanese *tanka* poet. These cluster around the first poem by a native English speaker. Jaime's voices catch more of this mix than any West Coast writer before or after.

What about West Coast fascination with primitive mind? I don't think anyone has been so insistent as Jaime de Angulo that what we regard as civilized mind is not an advance but a taming, a retreat. A diminishment of primitive mind. Probably connected to this gnawing and ransacking of consciousness has arisen a distinct strain of belief—among some—that poems regularly come from outside the poet. We have ample testimony that West Coast poets find songs or poems *out there*—in the rough canyons and oak covered hillsides. Is this the "New Western" poetics? Gary Snyder's "How Poetry Comes to Me"—

> It comes blundering over the
> Boulders at night, it stays
> Frightened outside the
> Range of my campfire
> I go to meet it at the
> Edge of the light

The most uncompromising believer in a poetry that arrives from *outside* is Jack Spicer. In contentious, half-drunk inspiration—you find it in his talks and lectures— he spoke of Martians visiting the poet, arranging the "furniture" of the poet's mind, & leaving their alien communiqués. In a lecture spurred by Cocteau's film *Orphée* he conceived the poet as a radio, receiving messages from outside. It is not the radio's business to ask where the message comes from or what it says, only to clearly receive it. Curiously, Spicer in the late forties did private tutorials with Jaime in San Francisco. According to Robert Duncan they worked on linguistics. I have no sense how closely the two worked, or where their conversations ranged, but Spicer did co-author a serious linguistic article early on. Notebooks or letters of Spicer's from those days may eventually surface, and show clear links to this West Coast tendency. An undated letter Jaime wrote Ezra and Dorothy Pound in 1950—

> I HAV met a few   very few non INJUNS
> in California capable of intelligent approach. frinstance,
> there is a young fellah named Jack Speicer (or is
> it Speiser?)

> ditto an old fellah named Rexroth

In the final year of de Angulo's life, the poet Robert Duncan lived in the Berkeley Hills house, as the private secretary. Duncan had gotten in touch at Ezra Pound's urging. He typed up Jaime's huge, still unpublished book *What Is Language?* and helped with the *Old Time Stories* manuscripts, with their fonetik spelling and scatter of linguistic symbols. In 1976, talking with Bob Callahan, he spoke of Jaime's "constant fascination with what was a shaman." Duncan adds, "I have a very pronounced pelt on my back and neck, and Jaime told me immediately that I would qualify in the Sur territory for a wer-bear, and he was fascinated because in my poetry bears had already appeared."

This manner of speaking—"in my poetry bears had already appeared"—lies in the direct tradition of Jaime's "I have unintentionally dropped into the manner of speech of my Pit River friends." It is a very modern and a very old belief about the origins of poetry, a belief about territory in which creatures of luck, power, medicine, call it what you want, walk through our songs. A belief that gives a wry squint at psychology's effort to reduce it all to the human unconscious. Might it be that wilderness—wild ecosystems—are the true unconscious?

But here we enter a mystery best left for the world of the poem. A world where beings of spiritual power make gifts if you are brave or reckless enough to seek them out. A world where bear, coyote, locust or fox may appear with unforeseeable counsel. Where they might say, *When you want me, you come here and sing my song. I'll hear you. I'll come.* A world where the one indispensable power is to know a few songs.

1. Someone pointed out that the equally eccentric, hard working, and decidedly secretive ethnographer James Peabody Harrington knew this world as well as de Angulo. Harrington compiled thousands of cartons of notebooks and documentation of California Indian languages, which he stashed so many places that nobody really knows how much work he accomplished. That's a story for another day.

Hand stencils, Chauvet Cave

Towards Arcturus

I

EARLY ON THE MORNING OF OCTOBER 10TH, 2005, the telephone rang. It was still dark, the fire had gone out, and the house was extremely cold. Alice was on the line. "I can only speak for a moment. Your father has just received the Nobel Prize in Economics. He's doing up his tie and we are off to a press conference." Before I could reply my father's wife hung up.

A few weeks earlier I had been walking the flanks of South Arapaho, in the Indian Peaks Wilderness, with my partner Marlow. We had ascended through fir and spruce to Diamond Lake at 11,000 feet, made tea on a low, east-facing outcrop, and sat looking across the lake to stark cliffs and jumbled talus. I was voicing some emotion about my father when Marlow interrupted. "Write a poem for him. Tell him just what you are saying to me. Talk to him in a poem." Her words threw me into turmoil. It took an hour on the trail to clarify for myself the following thoughts.

I cannot make poems out of the language I speak. To me a poem arrives as a configuration of energy, images, and impulses, closer to a vision than to a set of words or ideas. It contains its own intelligence and metabolism. It has little to do with what I personally might wish to say, though occasionally in the poem I will find a way to work in certain thoughts I could hope to articulate. Perhaps a poem for me is like hearing the tune of a song to which I must now carefully fit lyrics on a theme determined by the composer. Half the lyrics will be nonsense except within the field of the poem, within the specific range where it casts a glow.

This is not accurate. The best I can do is to recall that certain Indian traditions of North America speak of the song as a visitation, or a gift from outside. Regularly it is an animal spirit that delivers the song, which then lends the person its power. What *I want to say* may be part of the feral instinct that confers the song, but should I try to make a poem say what I want, power seems to depart on unseen feet.

It seemed impossible to tell my father of my love for him in a poem.

I study the Hunter's Moon as it moves towards dawn above North and South Arapaho Peaks. By late October the invitation has come to travel to Stockholm, to watch the King of Sweden confer the medal on my father. I am about to write, as in a kind of journal, impressions of this man my father, of Stockholm, and of the circumpolar North. This record will acquire whatever value it can from an edgy watchfulness, from the presence before my eyes of what is mysterious, animated, and fragmentary.

The award is for his applications of game theory to a series of social and political problems. My brother tells me that in an interview, when asked why he had turned to economics our father replies, "I grew up during the Great Depression of 1929. I thought what I wanted to do with my life was to understand how a financial collapse had come about, and as the most devastating event of my childhood try to prevent such a thing from recurring." By the early nineteen-fifties when he began his independent work, a post-war economy had created a completely different set of circumstances. The immediate and dramatic peril during the Cold War period was the proliferation of nuclear weapons. Thomas Schelling discerned a way to make discussion more sane, more accurate—to understand the minds of those who control the weapons—by applying a calculated model of conflict and cooperation.

When I was eleven I asked for a rifle for my twelfth birthday. My mother and I quarreled daily at the time, and my father promised me a gun on January 14th if I could manage thirty days without speaking rudely to my mother. I held my tongue with proud restraint and went a week before the old quarrel erupted. Starting over I managed perhaps five days. I went to my father and said, "I cannot make it thirty days without getting angry at her. But this should have nothing to do with owning a gun. I

Thomas C. Schelling, early 1940s

can be responsible and safe and treat a gun with respect. My disagreements with my mother are another matter." He sat in silence for a while and then said, "You're right, your relationship with your mother has nothing to do with a gun." We went to a sporting goods store and bought a .22 rifle the morning of my birthday.

Having read about it somewhere, having studied a bit of the literature, talked to friends in Germany and Scotland, I have gone around telling acquaintances that no bear has inhabited Europe for four hundred years. Now a guidebook informs me that nearly 1000 brown bear (*Ursus arctus*), what in this country we call Grizzly, live in the forests and mountain regions of northern Sweden. Once hunted nearly to extinction—not sport, not for its meat, fur, or medicinal value, but tracked down because of occasional depredations on reindeer—their population has increased in recent decades thanks to strict conservation measures. Brown bear are slowly reentering the south part of the country, and their range stretches northwards to above the Arctic Circle. That of course is the circle of The Great Bear, and I cannot speak the name without feeling a surge of excitement that makes my heart race. I think of the circumpolar bear cults documented by travelers across the planet's boreal regions: Siberia, northern Europe, the forests of North America, and among the Ainu people of Hokkaido, Japan's northern island. All have had a cult of the Bear.

During the last glaciation the Cave Bear (now extinct) frequented the limestone caverns of southern Europe. The climate of the Mediterranean was then much more like Scandinavia today, the tundra ecosystem broken by conifer forests that dropped

Bear skull altar, Chauvet Cave

down to the Mediterranean shoreline. In Chauvet Cave, discovered in the Ardéche region of France in 1994 by a group of adventurous cavers, and named for one of the discoverers, there is a Hall of Bears, each image exquisitely fashioned in charcoal and manganese. Piles of Cave Bear bones litter the floor; a bear skull placed 30,000 years ago on a block of stone fallen from the roof has invited speculation by archaeologists, scholars, and poets. Bears used to scrape their claws along the porous walls of the district's caves, and some folk wonder if their graffiti might have led humans to begin scraping images into the same walls. Bears could be ancestral teachers of human image making. I must ask Clayton Eshleman about this.

From Germany Stefan Hyner writes, "Well these brown bears here (*Ursus arctos*) are *brown bears*, about 10 feet tall & some 700 kg they're pretty much the size of a grizzly. By the way there are some left in the Balkans that cross over into Austria, Rumania & Hungary every once in a while, & the last one in the Pyrenees was killed last year or so, tho some people say there's still a population in remote areas."

When I waken Althea October 10th with news of her grandfather's Nobel she leaps out of bed waving her arms in excitement. I realize that even to the young the award has a nearly mythic standing, made all the more mysterious to Americans by virtue of it being conferred by a King who remains remote in his frozen kingdom of the aurora borealis. In fact, I cannot recall having seen an image of Sweden's king, and know nothing of his powers or authority except that he awards the Nobel laureates their prizes.

Later that day Althea exclaims, "Dad—it's bigger than the Grammies!"

Whatever skills I command as a storyteller—in fact my love of storytelling—comes from my father. My childhood was an ongoing cycle populated with animal characters. Beyond the immediate members of my family these must have been the most real people I knew, full of quiet instruction, playfulness, and the kind of sage circumspection I detect, now that I am grown, in my father's own speech. As an adult I have not thought to ask where his stories came from. They are unlike anything I have read in a book, though their cast of characters—their pantheon—is close to hand. The animals of his stories were simply the smaller wild fauna and intimate birds of North America. Blue jay was constant, and I remember badger, a rabbit named Maximillian, and a mole. Could pine marten have gone among them? The vivid figure, the center of the cycle, was prairie dog, sagacious, mysterious, with a knack for being around when anyone needed help. It now occurs to me that the landscapes of my father's stories, what I have come to call bioregions, were those of the American West. The West's animals are strangely named. I have always known that prairie dog is not a dog. He is far wiser, far more foolish, and way more elusive than any dog. He is not coyote, no, but in the stories my father told he carries some of the prairie wolf's enigma, inscrutability, proclivity to show up at unexpected moments, and homegrown ingenuity.

Prairie dog knows how to use something coyote never asked for. He uses it in my father's stories to solve nearly any dilemma. *Two sticks of wood.* "If I had two sticks of wood I would take care of this," would send the little animals scampering in search of juniper twigs. It was never clear to me what he did with those two sticks, but they were indispensable to his solution of the problem.

Thomas Schelling has—

"...contributed to enhancing our understanding of conflict and cooperation. [He] has achieved this by extending and applying game theory—a method used to analyze strategic interaction among different agents.

[His] work has transformed the social sciences far beyond the
scope of economics ... Schelling's research continues to shape the
debate on the formation of social institutions."

PRESS RELEASE 10 OCT 2005
THE PRIZE IN ECONOMIC SCIENCES.
THE ROYAL SWEDISH ACADEMY OF SCIENCES.

The release goes on to say, "In the mid-1950s, Thomas Schelling began to apply
game-theory methods to one of the era's most vital issues—global security and the
arms race. As Schelling himself noted, considerable progress can be achieved simply
by drawing a diagram which describes the alternatives available to the opponent and
one's own country, followed by a systematic consideration of the outcome in different
cases."

It occurs to me that I've never looked at one of these diagrams. How complex are
they? On the *MacNeil/Lehrer NewsHour* he says to an interviewer, "If I had a black-
board and a piece of chalk I could teach you how to do this in an hour."

Two sticks of wood, I think.

II

"Tracking is where science and storytelling join."
Mark Elbroch, *Mammal Tracks and Sign*

THE CIRCUMPOLAR ARCTIC COMPRISES ONE CONTINUOUS ENVIRONMENT OR
BIOREGION. In A. Irving Hallowell's justly famous 1926 essay, "Bear Ceremonialism
in the Northern Hemisphere," the region is the original site of the earliest bear cults,
referred to as circumpolar, or hyperborean: "above the taiga." These days degradation

of the Arctic is part of most people's thinking, popularized by accounts of melting polar icecaps. The worldwide elevation of sea levels takes on animal-mythic dimension when accompanied by talk of the threat to polar bears. Conservation biologists say that with the loss of ice, polar bears are subject to rapidly diminishing habitat, must travel farther for food and shelter, and their food sources could vanish entirely.

"Some [Arctic peoples] are skeptical of anthropologists," Lani Abbott writes to me, "just as Native peoples in North America are. There seem to be lots of Swedish social anthropologists—must be the lack of poetry in their souls, as the Norwegians like to joke. Anyway, Scandinavians like to count things and from the bibliographies I've seen, they must have accounted for every birch leaf by now." Wondering where the name Scandinavia comes from I go to *The American Heritage Dictionary* and find Scandi a Latin term, applied by Romans to the hyperborean lands, "an ancient and poetic name."

December 5

Arrived by Scandinavian Airlines about 7:45 a.m. with Marlow and Althea. Immigration flashes our passports under a scanner and waves us through. There is no visible customs officer. The airport looks almost Japanese in its spare elegance. The architect was exclusively interested in design or form, so the building's grace comes from its lines. It is without ornament, the floor is wood, and only looks dingy by the toilets, which you enter through a wall of riveted gray steel. We ride by taxi towards Stockholm, passing through the remnants of conifer forest. The woods have been cut back to make room for corporate buildings and parking lots. The corporation names look familiar, cut into angular modern glass and steel. I intend to put in as much effort as possible, learning about Sweden's wilderness; about the Sami people who I imagine to hold a trove of information about their bioregion, contained in the grammars and word-hoards of their speech; about the reindeer, emblems of the Arctic region, half of them wild, half domestic, like hoofed messengers between the forest spirits and the towns.

By the time the taxi drops us in Stockholm—"tree-trunk island"—it is raining and seems to be getting dark. When I unpack I find U.S. security has gone through my suitcase. They have confiscated the matches from a waterproof container in my survival kit. Why did I bring the backcountry survival kit (knife, flashlight, matches, sun block, SPF lip balm) when what I need are a tailcoat and white tie?

The Grand Hotel has housed Nobel Laureates and their families since the prize was first issued. Its wide, understated stone facade faces the "brackish" water, in from the sea, over which business-like boats and tugs push. On the other side of us the water is sweet. The guidebook says it has drained down from Lake Mallaren, and holds yachts, restaurant boats, and sightseeing watercraft. Directly across the brackish water, on the old-town island of Gamla Stan, stretches the Royal Palace, reputedly the largest inhabited palace in the world. Its residents descend from a Germanic people that moved into the region ten or eleven thousand years ago as the glaciers withdrew from Europe, when meadows and forests began to open up, emerging in the meltwater of retreating ice.

About that same period the first Sami people entered the northern part of Scandinavia, arriving from the east, present-day Siberia, following the reindeer. The reindeer, changing their old routes, were following the emergence of green plants from retreating ice, as they do every year in their migrations. Only this particular period, the close of the last glaciation, drove the decisive migration of our own recent history. It ushered in the Holocene. The Sami carefully guard, or did until recently, a "song of the plains," the *joik* or *jojk*, a song which belongs to an individual and in some way "carries or expresses that person's spiritual essence." Certain locations—power spots—also get held in a *joik*, as do certain animals. For a North American who has learnt to read poetry outside the English departments, or who has made a study of archaic traditions, this sounds familiar.

At dinner at the Naglo Restaurant, down a narrow cobbled street from the hotel—dimly lit with candles, long intimately furnished tables with white cloths that barely glow in the dimness, rich carpets and side-boards of burnished wood—Tom and Alice describe getting news of the Nobel. Twenty family members are present at one table, including all four of Tom's sons and six of his eight grandchildren. Everyone leans in to listen. The Nobel Committee, Alice recounts, will disclose nothing of their deliberations until the formal morning announcement, October 10th, when they release the name or names of their selection in Economics to the press. Shortly before the press gets word, the Committees contact those who will receive the award. The Committee tried to contact Dad but had a wrong telephone number, and it took them hours to locate the right one. The call, Alice says, came in shortly before 7:00 a.m. to their Bethesda home. By then the announcement had gone out to the press. The next call came from Bratislava, Slovenia, moments after the Nobel people had hung up.

> Alice: "The Bratislava intelligence agency is better than the Swedish. They found us faster."

> Dad: "Swedish intelligence could have found me by consulting a Washington area phone book."

Moments later the phone rang again. A newspaper in Bogotá.

Along with the congratulatory letters came requests for autographs. Over the nine days we spent in Stockholm, a small, determined cluster of autograph seekers huddled in trench coats, anonymous dark caps, and wool mittens, near the Grand Hotel's revolving brass and glass front door. When a black Volvo limousine arrived the doorman would meet it, and men, always men, would separate from the shadows along the hotel's façade and glide onto the sidewalk holding out photos to be signed. The Laureates took their celebrity with amusement or dignity or both. Years ago Dad told me he'd received a letter: "Dear Thomas Schelling, Would you send me your autograph? This is in case you ever get famous. Then I can sell the autograph for a lot of money. Yours sincerely." He told me at the time he might write back, "Dear Sir, That is an unhappy request you have made of me. I will not permit myself to be used in such a manner, and cannot possibly comply. Yours sincerely, [signed] Thomas C. Schelling."

Game Theory does not solve problems. It serves to illuminate the nature of a problem. Who are the parties involved? What are the possible outcomes? What do the different parties hope to get? How much do they trust or mistrust one another? How do they understand others who have very different motives or needs from their own? Many of the newspaper reports catch our father saying that he gathered invaluable insights by negotiating with his children.

Between dinner and coffee at the Naglo I asked Dad, down the long table, about the stories he told Tommy and me when we were children. It occurred to me I had never thought to find out where he got them. Had he drawn on stories he once heard? Did his own father tell similar tales? Had he worked off characters found in story-books? The name Maximillian had come at my urging I think, from a rabbit in one of my picture books. Did he now, in Stockholm in 2005, remember the stories he told in the late fifties, what specific plots or enigmas he worked into them? Does he even recall what animals tracked through the bedtime hours? He looked puzzled. My youngest brother, Robert, was born in 1960, so it may have been forty years since Dad had told one of his sons an animal story.

We'd been drinking wine and eating for a long time. The cobbles of the dark street, wet from Stockholm's mild winter rain, looked phosphorescent out the large window. Nobody walked the street. There were no cars. The brackish water and the sweet were pitching about—and it's possible global climate change is the reason there are no ice skaters this year on the system of waterways that binds the separate islands of Stockholm. There were no streetlamps; cobblestones caught their luminescence from far off lights. I wondered if the moon as well as the sun makes only the scantest appearance this far north in winter. Dad seemed barely able to recall the childhood stories, as if I'd asked about a dream he'd told years ago. I started to remind him of Maximillian and Prairie Dog, but Michelle chirped in with a bright intelligent voice. She is the wife of Karl Anderson, Dad's Nobel attaché, a tall Swede with degrees in public policy. Michelle also studies policy. She says with great intensity that *The Strategy of Conflict* was her bible, both as an undergraduate in the States and as a graduate student. She is American, younger than any of Dad's children. She speaks with wide, admiring eyes and an effortlessly sculpted vocabulary. What she says seems impossible to me. For the first time, Dad's entire family regards him in a new light. Young women consider his book a bible.

That night I dreamt a bright turquoise lake on a forested mountain.

, For dinner later that week the women order various dishes. Robert, Miles and I order "Rentrilogi," reindeer trilogy: a small steak with biting wild game flavor, better than venison back home, a length of spicy sausage, and a narrow slice of liver, which I've heard can be "read" for the character of the butcher who cut it.

The Grand Hotel serves smoked reindeer meat for breakfast, sliced very thin, with a lingonberry jam. In a seasonal open air Christmas market around the corner on Stallgatan, several booths run by Sami sell reindeer hides and cuts of dried meat. The coat of a reindeer is long, unbelievably thick, and each of its underhairs is hollow. This is what keeps the animal—or anyone who wears coat, boots, hat, and mittens made of the hide—alive at temperatures as low as minus 96° Fahrenheit.

> Its coat was so deep that I could run my fingers through it and
> hardly feel the solidity of the body beneath, but for all its depth the
> fur was neat rather than shaggy, with a rich, smoky smell ...
> Piers Vitebsky, *The Reindeer People*

Even in the open-air market, where 55 gallon drums filled with oak and birch are blazing against the whitish December air, you smell pungent reindeer hide at great distances. One wooden booth has cheese for sale; it's of reindeer milk, cured in some kind of whiskey.

Over the brackish water, near the summit of the island of Gamla Stan in a cobbled courtyard, is another Jul (Yule) season street fair. The booths sell mittens, hats, porcelain and glass Jul ornaments, bottles of spice for mulled wine, hand made cheeses, and tin or silver trinkets. Sami-operated booths draw no special attention. These sell cuts of dried reindeer meat, traditional steel knives, the blades short, thick and slightly curved, with handles of sectioned antler and birch. There are also flints embedded in antler thorn, reindeer-fur mittens, reindeer-hide boots ornamented with black, green, or red felt, and drinking cups with long handles carved of a single piece of birch. The upscale curio stores that line the winding streets sell glass reindeer, and a thousand tiny folk art trinkets, glass, ceramic, paper, or metal. Is the origin of the trinket, the chotchki, the doo-dad, to be found in the power object or amulet, now hopelessly distorted by market Capitalism and the overproduction of sentimental items? Little glass Santas, angels, trolls, gnomes, North Stars, and painted mushrooms. Red and white *Amanita muscaria* mushrooms.

The circle of people around the Nobel ceremonies is small. I find no Sami among them. When I inquire about Sami culture of the Caucasian Swedes they generally seem bemused that anyone's interested. This includes students at the University, staff of the Nobel organization, a woman named Joron who is Buddhist and has lived in Japan learning to produce the ceremonial Japanese braidwork that ornaments swords and military or imperial uniforms. Table companions at the Stockholm School of Economics also assume expressions of puzzlement. When I ask if Sami have a similar status in Sweden to the Indians in North America nobody understands. I did learn that scholarships are not established for Sami people, nor is there any affirmative action policy at the Universities. When I asked if young seekers from Stockholm or Uppsala visit the Sami to learn something of the Old Ways, of a pre-Christian religion, or of the archaic encounter with nature, animal spirits, and shamanic lore, Joron the weaver of ceremonial Japanese braids puts on a strange abstract look, then furrows her brow: "Maybe a few of the New Age sort." A whispered rise in tone turns her reply into a question.

At the School of Economics someone told me that the Sami, being nomadic, have no traditional land. Nothing like tribal allotments, reservations, rancherias, or autonomous zones, the types of land holdings that appear prominent in other parts of the world, especially in the States and Canada. The public land they range across with their half-wild herds is also required for timber, mining, gas and oil, skiing, conservation, and tourism, so a conflict underlies relations between majority Swedes and the Sami. Piers Vitebsky writes of "industrial ranching," and says, "Over the past fifty years the Sami people have transformed their traditional reindeer techniques into a technically sophisticated modern ranching system. Distances in Scandinavia are relatively small, and infrastructure highly developed." As in North America, the pressure on public lands between ranching and its competitors is acute. Hardly anyone in Stockholm sounded sympathetic to the reindeer herders.

I came from America thinking the Sami were Sweden's Indians. I'd had it backwards. "They're not the Indians, they're the fucking ranchers!" My question made no more sense than if I'd been inside the beltway in Washington and asked guests at a dinner party, "If your children have a spiritual hunger for their land and want to learn about the Old Ways or to attune themselves to nature, do they go to Wyoming and apprentice with a cowboy?"

III

THE NOBEL AWARDS CEREMONY OCCURS IN THE STOCKHOLM CONCERT HALL. The Swedish royal family, the Nobel laureates, previous recipients of the Nobel Prize, and assorted ambassadors, prime ministers, and dignitaries from mostly European countries take seats in a crescent on the stage. The stage is lush with icy white flowers, green foliage, twisting green vines, & a rich blue carpet. The scene looks like a Nordic fantasy world of ice and forest. If my father & the other Laureates—all men—had arrived at their seats borne on a reindeer-drawn sledge alongside a blonde sorceress in reindeer pelts, I wouldn't have blinked.

King Carl XVI Gustav presents the award medal to each laureate at the center of the stage, after the head of the appropriate committee has delivered a brief speech detailing what work the award is based on. Harold Pinter, the literature winner, has sent a surrogate to receive his award. He is in England ill with cancer, but delivered by video his lecture, a blistering attack on the Bush White House and its manipulation of language. The laureates for each of the other prizes sit in a crescent to the left side of the stage. After the awards in Physics, Chemistry, Literature, and Medicine—the subjects for which Albert Nobel had left his bequest—Dad rises and steps towards King Carl to receive diploma and medal for Economics. Stately in their formal tails, taking confident strides the two meet mid-stage, directly atop the large yellow-white N for Nobel, fitted into a circle on the Nordic or midnight blue carpet.

The two men, King and Laureate, stand upright in tailcoats and starched white collars. They bow slightly, from the waist. The Nobel diploma and the Nobel Economics medal in its flat square box pass formally from the King's left hand to my father's, beneath their clasped right hands. Dad then steps away from Carl XVI Gustav and moves slightly forward on the stage. He stands for a moment, in his own world, peering past or through the audience with a faraway gaze. His eyes are so deep, so darkly abstracted I wonder if he is staring, not at the Stockholm environment, but down the chilly corridor of the Cold War—the sixty year corridor that twists away from Hiroshima, through all the moments when nuclear warheads might have been used on a civilian population but were not.

In his Nobel lecture, "An Astonishing Sixty Years: The Legacy of Hiroshima," Thomas Schelling had spoken of the nearly mystical aura that has developed around the bombings of Hiroshima and Nagasaki. With each passing year those two occurrences reveal the eruption into history of a force beyond human comprehension; and he discusses a taboo—the word conveys some of the magical or religious fear—that has arisen around the use of nuclear weapons. Somehow those bombings, sixty years in the past, have become central to the spiritual life of humanity.

With his gaze held to the United States, he provided a brief history of the see-sawing approach to weaponry by American White House administrations. He quoted President Eisenhower on the military use of nuclear warheads in 1954 and 1955: "I see no reason why they shouldn't be used exactly as you would use a bullet or anything else," "...as available for use as other munitions."

By contrast, Tom Schelling invoked those who regarded the use of thermonuclear weapons as a nearly unthinkable escalation, their deployment nearly beyond the pale for a head-of-state to authorize. Lyndon Johnson in 1964: "Make no mistake. There is no such thing as a conventional nuclear weapon. For nineteen peril-filled years no nation has loosed the atom against another. To do so now is a political decision of the highest order." It can only be hoped, my father concluded, that the global community will collectively hold nuclear weapons taboo, now that India, Pakistan, North Korea, Israel, South Africa, hold such weapons in their arsenals, and in a short while will be joined by Iran. He closed by urging Congress not to miss the chance to adopt a new Test Ban treaty, to give the taboo a formal imprimatur. For an instant I glimpsed how Michelle could have read and reread his book as a "bible."

At the awards ceremony in the Concert Hall no secrets get revealed. The Laureates' names have been announced over the course of two weeks in October and newspapers throughout the world have profiled them. The laudatory speeches that precede the transfer of the medal between King and scholar have been published in a bilingual program, Swedish and English, and had been released early enough that foreign news media would have time to translate them. The awards ceremony—which has honored Rabindranath Tagore, W.B. Yeats, Samuel Beckett, and Yasunari Kawabata, among the writers I have read with care—is but a prelude to the great event, the Nobel Banquet. The most closely guarded secret of the Nobel week's affairs, the one every Swedish citizen will learn tonight, is the banquet's menu. The other secret, less speculated on but kept with equal secrecy, is the nature of the entertainment.

When the formal proceedings have finished everyone who attended the awards ceremony walks out of the Concert Hall and crosses a cobbled square in the drizzle. We file into buses in the rain. A relaxed police cordon rings the square. Beyond stand onlookers, with torches that flare against the light-hued yellowish stone buildings, holding a respectful vigil. Flames dart across the dark cobblestones. The crowd, several ranks deep, is silent. The buses remove us to the Stockholm City Hall for the banquet.

The City Hall was built by Ragnar Östberg between 1911 and 1934. Östberg took inspiration from Renaissance models, and his design displays not a touch of irony. It is so retrograde & dignified that it seems to mock the vigorous, erotic, quizzical architecture I associate with Europe in the era of industrial High Modernism following the First World War.

The Stockholm City Hall is constructed around two squares or piazzas, originally open-ceiling I am told. At some point the squares got closed over with roofs. The Nobel banquet takes place in the Blue Hall—named because it was to be painted Nordic blue. But the brick walls with designs raised elegantly in a rough dark reddish brick, the columns, arches, and soaring gallery windows lining the upper deck, the ceiling so far above that looking up you have the impression of seeing a cloudy sky—all looked so correct as it stood, the room never got painted. It is still red brick, with buff-grey stone, and to this day is known as the Blue Hall. It seats 1300 guests for dinner, and exists primarily for the December 10th banquet, which has been held there since Yeats spoke of " the great walls where the roughened surface of the bricks, their carefully varied size and tint, takes away all sense of mechanical finish." Yeats also thinks the workers who built it labored "as if they belonged to one family."

From *The Local*, Sweden's English language newspaper: "'Nordic' was the theme for this year's banquet in the Blue Hall." The same paper states that this year's menu is influenced by "Nordic wind," whatever that might mean. Perhaps my notes are scrambled, written in the hurried exultance of the event. Could it be Nordic wine? Nordic wand? Neither makes sense. The entertainment, too, is based on folk traditions, and in this context Nordic wind sounds promising.

However, each of the 1300 diners must first be seated in the Blue Hall, according to a meticulous plan, laid out both as lists and as diagrams in a formal booklet handed to us at the door.

Each table setting was built of an astounding number of plates and dishes, including a crescent-shaped dish for your bread and lidded tureen for the appetizer. The white China plates & saucers have Nobel rings of gold and teal green. There is a bewildering array of gold and silver eating ware. Before each setting stand four crystal glasses of different shape, for water, champagne, wine, and a liqueur. We'd seen Nobel banquet settings in several department stores and hotels around Stockholm, and a quick estimate put the cost at $300-400 U.S. for a single set. Uniformed college students in round white caps with tiny black brims and flying blue ribbons—making them resemble children dressed up as sailors—helped the 1300 guests into our proper seats. Some commander held the master chart, surely a complicated document, that told the master choreographer which guests could eat only vegetarian, who was allergic to shellfish, who had a lactose intolerance, who wouldn't eat bread, who was vegan, and above all, who was Kosher. My father's co-awardee in Economics, Robert Aumann, an Orthodox Jew from Israel, had brought his full clan. They sat at a table to themselves, the men black or gray bearded wearing their full-brimmed black felt hats, the boys curly-locked in sober yarmulkes, the women in tight, chaste bonnets.

"To the delight of the photographers, Princess Madeleine—who missed the gala last year because of a bout of 'flu'—was present this year, wearing a grey lace dress." *The Local* also reported that, "the evening provided a brief respite for Foreign Minister Laila Freivalds, who is under intense pressure to resign after her department was lambasted for its response to the tsunami catastrophe a year ago. She sat beside the economics prize winner, Thomas Schelling."

In the processional down the stone staircase—the stairs ample enough to accommodate four mounted Cossacks abreast in that old Peter the Great film of Czarist Russia—the heavily pressured Laila Freivalds had been steadied by my father's arm. She was his escort—a good choice, because my father has the ability to accept people without judgment, and to negotiate delicate matters of public concern with cool-headed dignity. I remember Daniel Ellsberg telling me that after he released the *Pentagon Papers* to the *New York Times* and *Washington Post*, of all his former colleagues only my father continued to receive him into his home and their friendship never faltered.

In a moment, after the dignitaries and royalty had taken their seats, everyone suddenly had sparkling white wine. However the master plan works, as a guest I never felt the intrusion of a waiter; yet everyone present seemed to receive champagne, wine or food at the same instant, and there was never a moment your glass sat empty. The best restaurants I have been to in the States cannot keep your wineglass full. Clearly it is not money, but excitement, national pride, intellectual elegance, perhaps Nordic "wind," that speeds the wine to your table.

The Allmanna Sangen Choir provided the entertainment. This too could be what the newspapers called Nordic wind. The Choir is Sweden's oldest university choir, from Uppsala. Abruptly—with a startling charge to the atmosphere—its members in an eruption of harmonizing voices spread above us in the galley, visible through Renaissance windows or between columns, crying out a Swedish sheepherder's call. Others flowed down the great stairway, clad in black and white, some wearing enormous floral headdresses, others bearing a tower or massive wand of flowers, all crying forth their energetic song-parts, revolving, bending their knees, shifting in wild circles, spreading through the hall until they surrounded the tables and dominated the overhead galley.

The men and women sang different parts, the men booming a low baritone, the women angelic or passionate, negotiating the upper registers. They whirled and circled in tight spirals about the long tables, the way reindeer collect when excited or panicked. The flowers were "dominated by lilies, roses, calla lilies, and carnations, in yellow, white, and red." Women in white gloves that fit tight to the biceps, snow-white wing-like starched shawls over one shoulder and breast; black blouses, white pleated skirts; they whirled past our table, dropping flowers into empty vases with teasing gestures I associate with the faeries in *A Midsummer Night's Dream*. "O Bottom, thou art translated!" Great animal bodies of young lads and pastoral lasses in their prime. And the tables became fantasy gardens of a Midwinter night's dream. Carmine and orange lilies, crimson roses, Nordic blue larkspur. The men in ivory jackets, many crowned with leaf and floral headdresses, circled at their deeper, baritone pace, grunting like reindeer do when they wind into tight counter-clockwise knots, tendons clicking over their ankles.

"Kept as secret as the menu," the 2005 performance was titled "Floral Transformations." The individual pieces were "Floating Flower Field Trip," "Decoration Delivery Dangerously Delayed," (which held enormous erotic tension as the girls swirled in their sexy white gloves, toying with phallic pillars of lilies, teasing the mouths of the table vases, not quite setting the flowers into the cool receptive shafts, then with the lightest of touches delivering them). And finally, the dizzying pastiche of folk dance and goat-herder's song, "Princess Primavera's Plantation Parade."

Later, during the intoxicated dancing of the Ball that went deep into the evening in a sequence of ballrooms upstairs, Althea spoke to a few Uppsala students from the choir. They had become human again. Flower headdresses and their great animal voices had been left downstairs. Most of them were graduate students in the performing arts, exhilarated and fatigued by the performance. One young man confided that many had ingested hallucinogenic mushrooms for the event.

Street lore I picked up in the States from an American of Swedish descent says that hallucinogenic mushrooms spring up on the droppings of reindeer. Just as in the American West psilocybin appears on cattle dung. "Fairy rings."

If you run an Internet search for reindeer and mushrooms you find dozens of websites. Their accounts are, not of psilocybin, but *Amanita muscaria*, the little mushroom seen everywhere in Russian and Nordic folk art. This mushroom is the well-known "toadstool" with a red cap covered by white specks or spots. It was used by sha-

Reindeer Stone, Mongolia

mans throughout the circumpolar North, grows under larch and spruce trees, and in the intricate tangle of pop drug-culture, kitsch marketing, and serious anthropology, is associated with flying reindeer, the red and white clothes of Santa Claus, and most intriguingly, with Santa's midwinter descent through the chimney. One account says that at Winter Solstice the shaman, dressed like the mushroom which he carries in his sack, enters everyone's winter house. Not through the door, which is buried by Arctic snow—but through the smoke hole—to distribute mushrooms to the family inside.

On a biting cold night just before solstice, in the street fair on Gamla Stan, that great rock island housing the Royal Palace and tangled with cobbled streets, I bought two porcelain figures, two or three inches tall, to give to Althea. One is a Santa—or perhaps a Swedish elf—with red robe and cap, white beard and cuffs; his comically ecstatic face turns upwards, searching the heavens for reindeer or visions. The other: a red-capped mushroom with white stem, white polka dots flecking its surface. The two figures seem interchangeable. Across the deserts and steppes of western Mongolia, reaching into the Altai Mountains, stand hundreds of 'reindeer stones,' some 3000 years old. "On these stones, the reindeer is depicted," writes Vitebsky, "with its neck outstretched and its legs flung fore and aft, as if not merely galloping but leaping through the air. The antlers have grown fantastically till they reach right back to the tail, and sometimes hold the disc of the sun or a human figure with the sun as its head. The flung-out hooves seem to represent more than just a leap; it is as if the artist has caught the reindeer in the act of flying through the sky in an association with the deity of the sun."

•

Sankta Lucia Day, December 13

Barefoot, her white gown cinched at the waist with a scarlet sash. Lingonberry vines twist through her flowing hair, and a crown of tall, white, burning live candles drifts in the pre-dawn dark. On a platter she carries coffee & Lussekatte, "Lucy Cat" or devil's cat, a soft bun flavored with saffron. From farmhouse to farmhouse, ethereal, almost unreal, she moves on slender saffron feet. Through Stockholm's streets, into the houses, hotels, & colleges, she steps, opening the Jul season. Her feet look chafed and red from the icy sidewalks. In recent years she is joined by maids, also in white gowns, though only she wears the headdress of living candles. Starboys in white robes follow her too, with high white conical hats. She was martyred, Saint Lucy, in Syracuse on the island of Sicily, around 300 C.E., for refusing a forced marriage, keeping herself pure for her bridegroom Jesus. Some accounts have Viking envoys carrying word of her north, into the boreal forest, though it may have been "berserkers," warriors clad in bearskin shirts, who spread her cult. Sweden prides itself on being at the forefront of gender equality.

They sing seasonal carols, each event beginning and ending with "Sankta Lucia." The ones who descend the winding iron staircase into the dining hall at The Stockholm School for Economics add a medley of Beatles songs to lighten the afternoon. "Sankta Lucia," originally an Italian tune, passing through Europe has taken new lyrics in the language of each country it moves into. The soft, slightly minor chorus of voices is dead-of-winter melancholy and return-of-the-sun hopeful. The Nobel Prize winners in Economics have given morning lectures in the small amphitheater upstairs. Dad never once uttered the phrase "game theory" but illustrated the complicated psychology—or is it dead simple?—by drawing on old Alfred Hitchcock TV episodes.

For lunch—over abundant white wine—the Prize winners sit by senior faculty and the School's president. I had a seat alongside a high-strung, pretty, Swedish journalist with fashionable clothes and boyish auburn hair, who lives in New York raising funds for Swedish organizations. She quickly looked bored at my questions concerning the Sami people. To my left was Örjon Sjöberg, who turned out to have watched the Sami carefully. With authentic concern he drew me a picture of the economics and recent historical changes in Sami life-ways. For several centuries the white Swedes suppressed Sami culture. Örjon's account made government policies sound parallel to official American treatment of indigenous tribes: suppression of the old religion (replaced by Christianity, mostly Lutheranism), outlawing traditional dances and singing, and a deliberate elimination of the language. Young children, forcibly separated from their families, were removed to boarding schools where they were forbidden to speak except in Swedish.

I put my question to Örjon, whether young people from the cities—the non-Samis—go to the herders for an inquiry into how one lives close to the natural orders. Does anyone keep the lore of animal magic or pass forward botanical knowledge? He responded with unexpected force, deploring the removal of children in previous centuries to schools where they were punished if they spoke their own tongue. "Think what will be lost if the languages die out. Their speech precisely fits the country's ecology. They have a hundred words characterizing different types of snow." I should send him Piers Vitebsky's paragraph from *The Reindeer People*—

> In observing the behaviour of this animal for millennia, the reindeer people have created what is surely one of the largest technical vocabularies in the history of human speech. One Eveny scholar has compiled a list of 1,500 words in his language alone that refer to the colour and shapes of reindeer, their body parts, harnesses, diseases, diets and moods . . . Given the thirty or more indigenous

languages across the Russian North today, and the various groups of Inuit and native American hunters of caribou in the American Arctic, there must exist tens of thousands of specialized words for talking about reindeer and their relationship with humans.

"Government authorities burnt the paraphernalia of the shamans," Örjon adds with narrowed eyes. "Drums and such things. Their costumes, animal images, head-dresses." Having studied photographs and line-etchings by early travelers through the Scandinavian north or across circumpolar Asia, I've seen figures clad head to foot in animal skins, a frame drum in one hand, paddle-shaped drumstick in the other. Reindeer antlers sprout from their skulls. Metal or bone talismans hang off their belts. Bear, wolf, reindeer, wolverine.

Today Sweden's reindeer are entirely owned by the Sami. The animals are, says Örjon, "half domesticated." Sometimes an animal will break from its herd, following instinct, and vanish into the wilds. No wild reindeer has ever joined a domestic herd however. In the Jul market a young Sami had told us his practice is to use every part of the butchered *ren*, though he described the ethos as though it were an ideal rather than actual practice these days. It would be difficult in the market economy of industrial ranching. Hides, leather, antlers (these latter shipped to East Asia where they are ground into aphrodisiacs), the liver, the hooves. Örjon eats reindeer meat, but his family objects to the gaminess.

The Sami have no land holdings. Unlike white Swedes, they may hunt without licenses, and without regard to season. They may not however take endangered species: wolf, wolverine, brown bear, and one other predatory mammal that did not make its way into my notebook. Sami frequently come into conflict over use of publicly owned land, particularly with timber interests and what Örjon calls "industry." Their language, of Finno-Ugraic stock, has two major dialects and many local vernaculars. All this, Örjon says, makes Sami identity complex. It cannot be based on land holdings, since they have no traditional tribal residence but range widely. Linguistic affiliation doesn't work either, since for decades children were forcibly enrolled in Swedish-only schools. The Old Ways religion has gone underground, and Lonely Planet's *Sweden* guide says the Sami are now entirely Christian. When I do an Internet search for the old song, the *joik*, the "song of the plains," which once held the essence of a person, an animal, or a place, it turns up a number of contemporary pop singers. A Sami website ignores the recording artists but cuts description of the *joik* short. "This is spiritual so we will not speak of it."

IV

If beauty is not a gateway out of the net we were taken in at our
birth, it will not long be beauty, and we will find it better to sit at
home by the fire and fatten a lazy body or to run hither and thither
in some foolish sport than to look at the finest show that light and
shadow ever made among green leaves.
W.B. Yeats

WILLIAM BUTLER YEATS RECEIVED THE NOBEL PRIZE FOR LITERATURE IN 1923. In "The Bounty of Sweden," the account of the journey he took with his wife to receive the award, he observes a longstanding commerce between Ireland and the Scandinavian countries (to which he includes Iceland). "Danes" is the encompassing term he uses for Scandinavians, though he focuses on the Swedish. Their presence in Ireland he traces back to Viking incursions and raids. Yet Swedish influence on Ireland goes back to earlier transactions, with tracks disappearing into the prehistoric past. Beneath the narrative of history, Yeats has tuned his ear to supernatural events, to animal visitors and the hidden ones, the invisible folk or "little people" of County Galway, who live just beyond the range of human sight.

My own thought runs off to older influences. Only partly accounted for are Ireland's standing stones, passage tombs, pre-Celtic wedge burials, and the rune-like Ogham inscriptions, each letter scored in stone being named for the leaf of a northern tree, shrub or flower. Also dimly fit into archaeological records are the circle forts (*raths*), stone axe heads, endless-knots or spirit tracks carved on Neolithic tombs, journey spirals, and stylized animals, probably bear and elk. More directly traceable to "Danes" are the high windowless needle-shaped stone towers—there's one at Kilmacduagh Monastery near Yeats's Thoor Ballylee home—built by Irish monks. The monks fled through a portal thirty feet off the ground, drawing the ladder up when "Danes" came to loot and burn their abbeys.

•

Ten days in December, 2005.

At 9:00 a.m. the first wash of amber light begins to soak across Stockholm. It settles on grand yellow and salmon colored buildings, which remind me of Paris except they lack the frivolous plaster ornaments set near the Parisian roofline. Slowly a hard white sun moves on the southeast horizon. It makes the choppy water glint with mercury. By noon dusk has set in. At 2:30 candles appear along the sidewalk in front of cafés, restaurants or clubs. At 3:00 it is dark. No pause to the round of Nobel events: conferences, receptions, concerts, interviews, press appearances, lunches, dinners, lectures, award ceremonies, balls, banquets. Dad is usually shaved and ready to go before daylight. Once or twice he meets my brothers and me after midnight for Scotch in the Victorian sitting room of the Grand Hotel, virtually our only time to gather as father and sons.

Hoards of autograph seekers. Swedish television broadcasts the banquet and ball, and if I can believe the newspaper, has been watched by everyone who could not secure an invitation or ticket to the event. Dad seems unfazed by the pace. He climbs into the black Volvo for a trip out to the ethnic suburb of Rinkaby (Americans would call it a development or ghetto), to take the place of Harold Pinter. Rinkaby grade-school children always invite the Literature Laureate out to their neighborhood of Middle Eastern shops and low-income housing for a Sankta Lucia festival, where they sing Jul songs and perform a play based on the new Laureate's life and writings. The children are Somalian, Egyptian, Lebanese, Nigerian, Eastern European, and Hispanic.

Alice is trying to protect Dad from exhaustion. He doesn't show any fatigue, arriving at the hotel lobby always in good humor. Somewhere along the way he learnt to conserve his vital force. Marlow observes how astoundingly sexy he looks, and is certain all the young women think so. He's relaxed and warm whenever he and I get a moment to speak or pose for a photograph, and invariably cheerful with his grandchildren. He begins to resemble a T'ai Chi master, tailcoat and white tie supplanting the Oriental robe and thin beard. He is being honored for his mastery of something invisible, some mysterious inward control of psychic resources—outwardly supported by no more than a diagram or two sticks of wood, like the wooden staves used in Aikido—to avert the military use of nuclear warheads. At eighty-four he is the oldest Nobel laureate in history.

Ray Glauber's son confides over Scotch one night, "My father's eighty years old. When he got the physics prize he was the oldest recipient. That lasted four days. Then the economics committee named your father."

The final event in Stockholm, a *Luciabal* (St. Lucy's Ball) at the University, is sponsored by the Nature Science Union. The Union's totem animal is the frog. A program speaks obscurely of *The Order of the Ever-Smiling and Jumping Little Green Frog*. Traditionally this Union hosts the laureates, the spouse or consort of each laureate, and whatever members of his or her family have lingered past the official events. Only Marlow, Althea, and myself of the Schelling clan remain. We feel like stragglers. I get fitted for another set of tails—having sent my first outfit back—along with white tie, trousers striped with black satin down the out-seam, suspenders, and the starched white militarist vest-front with its confounding ribbons and tabs. Marlow looks brilliant in a filmy russet gown covered with pale florets once worn by her grandmother, and Althea wears a black skirt slanted at the hem that makes me think of Barcelona. Everyone has remarked on the colorful inventive array of gowns, hairstyles, jewelry, shawls, smart jackets, and fashionable shoes the women wear. The men, everyone repeats, look like penguins. Under those precise trousers with knife-sharp creases, my black roper boots hold a trace of Colorado wilderness.

Alice escorts Dad, holding his arm, clad in a careful lavender suit beneath copper hair. The women suffer the most, needing to prepare a different suit or dress for each of a daunting number of functions. Once again the Laureates are seated at a table in their honor. Everyone knows tonight will carry a different weight of dignity. Students pack the long banquet tables in the union building, not much less elegantly set than the tables at the Nobel banquet. This hall however holds only a whisper of the Blue Hall's nobility. It is a well-disguised downstairs cafeteria, and lacks the Renaissance world of soaring space, sculpted by columns, grand stairwells, and overhead galleys. Most students paid for tickets long in advance. Because it is younger, and their formal clothes edged with postmodern skepticism, the crowd seems more volatile, more exhilarated, than the one that filled the Blue Hall.

Marlow, Althea, and I are seated near each other, students ranging along the table on both sides. Max, a dark-haired law scholar thirty-seven years old with impeccable English speaks kindly to Althea, then scolds her mildly for some fierce opinion she holds that he thinks childish. I'm next to Anna, editor in chief of the University newspaper. No longer a student but still in her twenties, she has a quicksilver laugh to go with what must be a watchful editorial presence at tonight's event. Her tight blonde pigtails look severe, yet pixie-like or mischievous against her slender neck and platinum gown.

At our table there is talk of politics, first over a clearcolored firewater, then over dinner and the very good French wine everyone drinks prodigiously. The meal started with venison carpaccio, paper thin on bitter green leaves. Platters of roast char came next, with asparagus and a potato-cheese dish. Finally a lime-scented crème with brandy poached pear. Our table partners were surprised at our outspoken leftist convictions, and remarked that we seemed current on world affairs. The Americans they meet on Stockholm's campus must appear insular, naïve, or conservative. We could not talk long though. With the disappearance of dinner plates a low stage took two spotlights and the proceedings began.

A sharply attired woman with poise and a whip-like humor, and a quick-witted man to serve her as foil, took the microphone. They were masters of ceremony, and their honoring of the Nobel laureates was a skilfully sharpened lampoon. Most of their banter came edged with contemporary affairs & gossip the Swedish knew from their daily papers but which regularly eluded us North Americans. At one point the woman on stage used the word bourgeoisie. When I laughed, Anna and Max and the others seated around leaned in. "What was that word?" "Bourgeoisie." "What does it mean?" Now I was surprised. These politically minded students—lawyers, journalists, and candidates for degrees in political science—seem without a basic vocabulary, or to have read no Marx, Engels, Lenin, Trotsky, or Che.

While I gave quick definitions of "bourgeoisie" and "proletariat" our table partners listened intently. Anna pointed to the lady MC. "She is the President of the Student Union." The others solemnly nodded. "She is a Communist."

We saw Dad and Alice rise and leave the room. They were due in Uppsala in the morning. What we did not know was that representatives of the Supreme Order of the Ever Smiling and Jumping Green Frog recognized Dad on his way out. Separating him from Alice they drew him into a side room and initiated him into their mysteries. Shortly afterward, the order descended the stairs behind the stage to enter the banquet room. Four of them bore on their shoulders an enormous green frog of papier maché. Its green textured skin blinked with red lightbulb eyes. Everyone rose and the room joined energetically in what I later learnt is a favorite Swedish folksong, "The Frog." During its staccato refrain, "kek-kek-kek-kek-kek-kek-kek!" everyone jumps rapidly up and down in unison.

Men in tailcoats, pressed trousers, white ties; women in costly gowns, coifed hair, bright jewels—springing upward and down on frog legs. I want to imagine that a trace of the oldest ritual, held by these people since the glaciers withdrew 10,000 years ago, had swept in with the papier maché frog totem. A shaman's frog dance, its original meaning nearly obscure, is repeated every year in this cafeteria. The dance of the springtime frog, mimed by the clan at winter solstice when the sun's power is entreated to return to the Northern taiga and waken the bogs and marshes that lie under deep ice. *Le Sacre du printemps!* I thought of the frog hymn in the *Rig Veda*, seeming so incongruous, a relict of beliefs that predate the Vedas, descended from a period when animals held the clue to our destinies, our poems imitated the bark of the deer, and frog was a notable emergence of the season's ritual calendar.

The evening proceeded quickly with each of the laureates—their discovery or contribution first parodied by the hosts at the microphone—being called up to the stage to repeat obscure mantras. This was their formal induction into The Supreme Order of the Ever Smiling and Jumping Green Frog, and the repeating of secrets that must never be spoken. Liquor had flowed; excitement rippled through the room; and perhaps English is alien enough a tongue, that the title of the order became fluid. The Order of the Supreme Jumping and Evergreen Smiling Green Frog. The Supreme Green Order of the Ever Smiling Jumping Green Frog. Was this deliberate? The way Northern game hunters once scrambled the names of prey as they passed up river drainages, or used precautionary epithets to deceive a malignant spirit that could interfere with the hunt?

Ray Glauber was called forth. "Ray Glauber has made significant discoveries in the use of fiber optics and light, for measuring minute increments of time. For most of us, however, in practical terms the smallest meaningful increment of time is 'the minute'. In Sweden the minute has many definitions, but the most accurate is 'the amount of time it takes Laila Freivalds to change her mind'." The hall erupted in laughter. What is this about? I asked, and under the roar Anna and Max and the others leaned towards us. We learnt that Sweden's slow response to last year's tsunami, after it destroyed the beaches in Thailand and left thousands of Swedish citizens dead, injured, or helpless, had horrified the populace. "Even Italy," the political science student told us—Anna swung her pigtails indignantly—"even Italy moved quicker. And we Swedes

think the Mediterranean people slow, disorganized, lethargic, wrapped up in red tape."
It had taken Freivalds a week to release Scandinavian Airlines jets to retrieve Swedish
survivors from the devastated Thai coastal areas.

"Nothing like this has happened before." Anna says. The political science scholar
adds, "Our last war was in 1812. No living Swede has seen a public disaster. We do not
have earthquakes or hurricanes." Someone tells me that 500 Swedes died when the
tsunami hit Thailand's beaches, and I remember television shots of blond children
eaten by the wall of seawater.

Now the honors had been conferred. The serious drinking was to begin. Up and
down the long tables everyone locked elbows and rocking left and right sang—

> Punschen kommer, punschen kommer,
> ljuv och sval.
> Glasen imma roster stimma
> I vår sal.
> Skål för glada minnen!
> Skål för varje vår!
> Inga sorger finnas mer,
> när punsch vi får!

The rocking became wilder, an almost violent counterpoint to the lyrics. A stray
thought came to me: at our table no poets … but I lost the thought as chairs were
kicked out of the way and we stood. You couldn't have remained seated, not with your
arms locked into the drinkers beside you.

While we sang the elusive thought slipped into view: Before descending to the
cafeteria banquet room there had been a brief reception upstairs. There was a chaste setting of small cups of *glug*—hot Jul wine steeped for days with currents & sprinkled with
sliced almonds—and *peppar kakor*, ginger snaps, traditional at Jul. I'd spoken with the
President of Stockholm University and asked about creative writing programs. He lis-

tened with interest as I described them in the States. He seemed to grasp the concept but nodded with studied concentration, "No, no, we have nothing like that in Sweden."

"Punch is coming, punch is coming!" An abrupt single force brought us to a stop, feet gripping the floor, then with a single motion wrenched us standing onto our chair seats, rocking with abandon, the women on precarious heels. You are not permitted to sit again until your 'punch' has arrived. Waiters hurried with glass beakers. Judging by the thick, squat cups set before us this punch might hold enough juice to draw the sun back from the south regions.

> Punch is coming, punch is coming,
> soft and cool—
> Glass is frosted
> in a hall—
> Skoll for happy memories!
> Skoll for everyone!
> All our sorrows chased away
> When punch has come!

Max translated the lyrics for us over the roar and I transcribed them onto a cloth napkin. As the University has no creative writing program there would have been no poet-in-training in the room. Only the presence of the ancient frog shaman, a sort of proto-poet. I was both moved and amused when I realized that among these scholars of law, physics, medicine, political science, and business, the celebration could not reach its climax without the aid of lyric poetry.

On our return drive to the Grand Hotel I calculated 1000 live candles in the windows of one residential apartment.

Tak för de gute maden.

18 December   Colorado, 12:30 p.m.

I just spoke with Dad. He has received many invitations to lecture overseas. One offer from Brazil he has turned down. An offer has come from Cuba, which he thinks he'll decline. "Why would you decline Cuba?" "I need to select carefully which offers I'll accept, and they must be willing to bring Alice," he tells me. "There are so many invitations." He listens carefully while I describe the *New York Times'* account of the World Games in baseball. The Bush administration has declared that Cuba's team will be barred from entering the United States. The U.S. embargo of Cuba permits no activity that might financially benefit Cuba or any of its citizens. Television or radio broadcast, the sale of merchandise with team logos, lodging or food provided by the Game sponsors, even publicity, will violate the embargo's terms. Under the Clinton administration, lawyers found clauses that allowed Cuba's team to play in the States. But the Bush White House—their eyes on donations and votes from Miami's conservative Cuban exile population—stands firm. Ballplayers and fans know the Games are a joke though, if the Cuban team doesn't compete.

Dad listens quietly. It is a long time since he and I attended a ballgame together. Then very slowly, "I would not mind defending myself in court for violating the U.S. embargo of Cuba. That is something I would be willing to challenge." The old Soviet Bear no longer holds any threat for Dad. How is it that George W. Bush, too young to remember the Cuban missile crisis with adult emotion, seems threatened that baseball might expose how outdated the embargo is?

I return to Vitebsky's *The Reindeer People* and find him greeted by an Eveny man: "Thanks for visiting me, in our bear-ridden corner." The Eveny term is *medvezhiy vgol*. "Bear-ridden." The phrase means backwater.

•

"with bow uncased and shaft upon the string"

In these notes—on my father, on conversations that took place in Stockholm, on thoughts of the Northlands—I've scouted around but not found unmistakable tracks leading where I hoped to go. "The proper homeland of the bear cult appears to be the northeast-European forests," writes Rhys Carpenter. The tracks I'd like to find would lead directly to the role played by animal tales in our efforts to move through significant crises. What I can do is to speculate that my father—without knowing it, since this would have been alien to his way of thought at the time—was working through his crucial discoveries around nuclear disarmament as he spun tales of prairie dog, Maximillian, and the other animals of my childhood.

Claude Lévi-Strauss in *La Pensée Sauvage* traces "the arts of civilization" to the Neolithic mind. This mind—known to anthropology through studies of kinship, totemism, folklore, archaic art, and taboo—worked with meticulous observations of nature, especially plant and animal species. Prehistoric people based their mental diagrams, and their rational categories of thought, on animal character. It is here that the "tens of thousands of specialized words for talking about reindeer" formed. Simple binaries—which I suspect resemble the diagrams of game theory—include creatures that fly or don't, creatures that move by night or that move by day, creatures that crawl or that stand. Possibly the profoundest application of 'savage thought' led to domestication—of the goat, the dog, the cow, the horse, the cat, the reindeer. No animal has truly been domesticated since the end of the last glaciation.

It does not take an anthropologist or mystic to notice that the oldest strata of mind still thinks in terms of animals. This is true historically—the Aurignacian cave art of the Dordogne, the Ardèche, and the Pyrénées, was fixed on the megafauna of glacial Europe. Psychologically it seems true that animals populate the deepest creative strata. Children study animals with "the butcher's instinct," fascinated with animal parts and animal names. I've read that people who ingest yage, the South American *ayahuasca* vine, see large cats, the chief predator of humans, even if they have never encountered one.

The most primal fear: extinction of oneself and one's family. Confronting it where would you go? To the most archaic strata of mind? I can only surmise that my father worked with grim urgency as the Cold War moved into crises and the weapons race heated, as the Soviets shipped nuclear warheads to Cuba. Would these events of the nineteen-fifties and sixties have delivered him to his own primal, creative faculties, looking for ways to negotiate? Do the original grottoes of thought get reached—I think Lévi-Strauss would say so—by following animal tracks? Did my father's stories, the ones he told his children, emerge not from books he had once read or tales told by his mother, but out of his intent study of Cold War armaments?

"Tracking is where science and storytelling meet," says the author of the field guide I use.

I suspect these speculations would be foreign to my father. I put them down because it may be that his systematic discoveries, those the Nobel committee honored, were formed in two parallel theaters. The first, the Cold War arms race. The second the world of prairie dog and his two sticks of wood. I am unable to say how, but I know my drive for poetry was formed in both these worlds. This would be familiar to many tribal peoples: the poem, the song that shows the way forward, comes from the world of animal spirits. As in a hero tale, a frog may lead one out of the dark.

•

In the Stockholm Concert Hall, the Royal family sits towards the front of the stage in a crescent of chairs to the audience's right. Their faces are markedly intelligent and heroic. Their postures, especially Crown Princess Kristina's, are classical, and impress us all by not wavering for the two hours it takes to complete the ceremony. The Nobel Laureates sit in a similar crescent of chairs to the left. Above them the vegetation: thick green foliage, leaf-filled vines, wreathes of evergreen, exuberant white flowers. The carpet is deep Nordic blue. Towards the front, a circle contains the ivory-colored N for Nobel.

When I study a photo of Sweden's King and my father I realize N is what the audience sees. For King Carl XVI Gustaf of Sweden approaching from the right, and for Thomas C. Schelling stepping forward to receive his medal from the left, the emblem under their feet would read—

This is a symbol cherished from childhood. The designers of L. Frank Baum's Oz books conceived it. It appears on the spine of the third in his Oz series and each subsequent title. It is a *yantra*, a magic symbol that leads a North American child into an alternate world where animals talk, where figures made of straw, tin, wood or pumpkin learn to think and to love. It is a world where the political order holds in equal regard anarchy, monarchy, Socialism, feminism, and trade unions. If one single symbol can take a literate American of the twentieth century to the depth of childhood longing, this must be it. On December 10th, the laureate and the King, watched through American eyes, step for a moment into a sphere in which Oz is the kingdom. I phone Dad, and tell him I wish I had taken my emerald glasses. When I call his attention to the Oz symbol he utters a bark of pure laughter. It is a laugh I remember with unstudied warmth from my childhood. Hearing it brings back those moments of storytelling, when he and I were linked in a moment of imagination and humor that was the purest of emotions. Those were the moments, past the reach of Cold Wars, nuclear weapons, the movement of troops into Indochina, when we became linked as though sharing a single spirit. Embraced by the old mystery of genetics, family, and love.

Over the telephone, still laughing, he says, "When my great-grandchildren ask, I'll tell them I'm receiving the Prize from the Wizard of Oz."

Born January 14th, 1953, at St. Elizabeth's Hospital in Washington, D.C., Andrew Schelling grew up in "Thoreau territory," west of Boston. Moved to Northern California in the early seventies, then Colorado in 1990. In 1992 The Academy of American Poets gave him their translation prize for *Dropping the Bow: Poems from Ancient India*. Student of the Arapaho language, he is active on land use issues, visits game drive walls in the high country, and lives within the "grammar of ecology" in the American West. He has published twenty books of poetry, translation, & essays. Recent titles include *From the Arapaho Songbook, A Possible Bag*, and *Love & the Turning Seasons: India's Poetry of Spiritual & Erotic Longing*. He teaches at Naropa University in Boulder, Colorado, & at Deer Park Institute in India's Kangra Valley. In 2013 he began to work with The Bay Area Public School of Oakland, which is "collaborative and free."

COLOPHON

Set in *Vendetta*, designed by John Downer, distributed by Emigré.
Vendetta can be classified as a Venetian Old Style typeface,
yet not so much a revival but a fresh reworking. With both
chiseled rusticity & a broad-nib calligraphic directness,
this font has that venerable feel of handbuilt skill.

Book design: JB Bryan

Singing Horse Press Titles

Charles Alexander, Near Or Random Acts. 2004, $15.00

David Antin, John Cage Uncaged Is Still Cagey. 2005, $15.00

Rae Armantrout, Collected Prose. 2007, $17.00

Rachel Tzvia Back, A Messenger Comes. 2012, $15

Julia Blumenreich, Meeting Tessie. 1994, $6.00

Norman Fischer, Success. 1999, $14.00

Norman Fischer, I Was Blown Back. 2005, $15.00

Norman Fischer, Questions/Places/Voices/Seasons. 2009, $16

Norman Fischer, The Strugglers. 2012, $15

Phillip Foss, The Ideation. 2004, $15.00

Phillip Foss, Imperfect Poverty. 2006, $15.00

Phillip Foss, The Valley of Cranes. 2010, $15.00

Eli Goldblatt, Without a Trace. 2001, $12.50

Mary Rising Higgins,)cliff TIDES((. 2005, $15.00

Mary Rising Higgins,)joule TIDES((. 2007, $15.00

Lindsay Hill, Contango. 2006, $14.00

Lindsay Hill, The Empty Quarter. 2010, $15.00

Karen Kelley, Her Angel. 1992, $7.50

Karen Kelley, Mysterious Peripheries. 2006, $15.00

Kevin Killian & Leslie Scalapino, Stone Marmalade. 1996, $9.50

Hank Lazer, The New Spirit. 2005, $14.00

Hank Lazer, N18 (Complete). 2012, $15

David Miller, The Waters of Marah. 2002, $12.50

Andrew Mossin, The Epochal Body. 2004, $15.00

Andrew Mossin, The Veil. 2008, $15.00

Paul Naylor, Playing Well With Others. 2004, $15.00

Gil Ott, Pact. 2002, $14.00

Ed Roberson, The New Wing of the Labyrinth. 2009, $15

Ted Pearson, Encryptions. 2007. $15.00

Andrew Schelling, A Possible Bag. 2013. $15.95

Susan M. Schultz, Dementia Blog. 2008, $15.00

Susan M. Schultz, Memory Cards. 2011, $15.00

Susan M. Schultz, She's Welcome to Her Disease
            [Dementai Blog Volume Two]. 2013. $15.00

Heather Thomas, Practicing Amnesia. 2000, $12.50

Rosmarie Waldrop, Split Infinities. 1998, $14.00

Lewis Warsh, Touch of the Whip. 2001, $14.00

Singing Horse Press titles are available from
the publisher at singinghorsepress.com
or from Small Press Distribution (800) 869-7553,
or at www.spdbooks.org.